A Celebration

of

Priestly Ministry

A Celebration

of

Priestly Ministry

CHALLENGE, RENEWAL, AND JOY
IN THE CATHOLIC PRIESTHOOD

Walter Cardinal Kasper

Translated by Brian McNeil

A Herder & Herder Book
The Crossroad Publishing Company
New York

Original publication: *Diener der Freude. Priesterliche Existenz—priesterlicher Dienst* by Herder Verlag, Freiburg, Basle, and Vienna 2007.

First published in the English language in 2007 in the United States by

The Crossroad Publishing Company
16 Penn Plaza — Suite 1550
New York, NY 10001

This book is set in 12/16 Centaur.
The display type is Bodoni Antiqua.

Printed in the United States of America

Library of Congress Cataloging-in-Publication Data

Kasper, Walter, 1933-
  [Diener der Freude. English]
  A celebration of priestly ministry : challenge, renewal, and joy in the Catholic priesthood /
Walter Cardinal Kasper ; translated by Brian McNeil.
        p. cm.
  "A Herder & Herder book."
  Includes bibliographical references and indexes.
  ISBN-13: 978-0-8245-2467-8 (hardcover)
  ISBN-10: 0-8245-2467-5 (hardcover)
  1. Pastoral theology—Catholic Church. 2. Church work. I. Title.
  BX1913.K37I3 2007
  262'.142—dc22
                                    2007007357

1 2 3 4 5 6 7 8 9 10 11 10 09 08 07

Dedicated
to the confreres
with whom I was ordained
and to the priests
whom I myself ordained
as Bishop of Rottenburg-Stuttgart

Contents

Author's Note

I am grateful to Professor Dr. Donato Valentini (Rome) and to my sister, Professor Dr. Hildegard Kasper, who read through my manuscript and made many helpful suggestions. I am grateful to Dr. Bruno Steimer and Dr. Ulrich Sander of Herder Verlag for all their work in preparing the publication of this book.

Translator's Note

Most biblical quotations are taken from the New Revised
Standard Version, © 1989, Division of Christian Education of the National Council of the Churches of Christ
in the United States of America, but occasionally a more
literal translation is given in order to bring out the
author's point.

1

Priestly Life:
Krisis and *Kairos*

A New Pastoral Situation

The fiftieth anniversary of my ordination to the priesthood has prompted me to look back and reflect on the
last fifty years—a whole half century. Many changes have
taken place in these years and decades, not only in my
own life and in the lives of those who were ordained with
me, but in the life of the church in general, and not least
in the dramatic course taken by world history. On the day
of our ordination, forty of us were ordained. Today, no
bishop in Germany would dare even to dream of such a
number of new priests. And so the obvious question is:
how were these fifty years, what remains of them, and
how will the future be?

Profound Change

In the Western world, the priestly ministry and the concrete shape of the church in central and western Europe are in a dramatic period of upheaval, as we see from the decreasing number of seminarians and ordinations in almost every Western country. Naturally, we must not look at these numbers in isolation. There has been a decrease, not only in the numbers of priests ordained and persons entering religious life, but also in the number of baptisms, church weddings, and laity who practice their faith and attend Mass—especially among children and young people. The church's life as a whole is in a state of upheaval. We can, of course, formulate this situation in positive terms: the church has begun to move, and she understands herself as a movement, as the people of God *en route*. It is also true that the ecclesial upheaval must be seen in the larger context of the rapid and comprehensive transformation of society in every sphere of life, and not least in the context of demographic changes.

When we ask what future awaits the church, we are often told that "the hour of the laity" has sounded, and this is certainly correct, since the laity live and work in the specific situations of our rapidly changing world. It is they who are the experts in the various spheres of life, and it is only they who can work as a "yeast" there, spreading the light of the gospel. This is their service; but if the laity are to serve in this way, they need pastors to accompany them on their path and give them spiritual orientation. They need priests. The self-understanding of the Catholic Church affirms that priests have a key role here. It is above all through the priest that the concrete existence of the church is perceived and made present in our towns and villages.

The deep discontinuities of the last few decades have not passed priests by, either in the way in which others perceive them or in their own self-understanding. Both of these have become uncertain and unclear in many ways, and fundamental questions are often posed about the service, the hierarchical office, and the lifestyle of the priest. It is the priests themselves who are most immediately affected by the upheaval and who sense it most clearly, and this has led many of them to give up hope. Priests thus need encouragement and recognition. I believe that the strengthening of their identity and motivation is one of the most important tasks facing us today.

There is no reason to throw in the towel. Even today, there are still many priests whose pastoral ministry has a powerful diffusion. Our situation is not different from that in the days of Jesus: many people today "are like sheep without a shepherd" (Mark 6:34), and there is an increasing quest for God and for a reliable foundation and orientation for one's life; people speak openly about such matters. We are not only witnessing the end of an old order; we are also witnessing new beginnings, sometimes hidden in the hearts of the many who have begun to look for God anew and who are hungering for a healthy spiritual nourishment and sometimes openly for all to see in the movements that bring renewal to parishes and religious orders, as well as in the new spiritual movements. Where pastoral direction and spiritual orientation are given, and pastors genuinely accompany their people, we need not worry about whether anyone will in fact take up this "offer"; on the contrary, people, whether young or old, are searching for genuine pastors, perhaps even more today than in the past.

Crisis and Krisis

This is why we should be careful about using the word "crisis." I prefer to understand it in the original meaning of the Greek *krisis,* which does not designate a collapse or catastrophe but rather a situation of upheaval in which decisions must be taken. This is why a crisis can be understood as a challenge or indeed as a God-given *kairos* in which we are summoned to understand our situation as a task to be shouldered. This means accepting the crisis and mastering it.

This is not the place for a comprehensive analysis of our contemporary world and its culture nor for a detailed description of the ecclesial situation in western Europe. Once, the church was in a real sense the church of an entire people, but this will soon be a thing of the past. Once, a Catholic milieu with clear borders existed, but this has almost totally disintegrated. Let me simply note that a new situation has begun for the church in Europe: the situation of a second mission. Far-seeing bishops and theologians in France and Germany had already pointed this out even before the Second World War, and once again after the total collapse in 1945. They spoke of France and Germany as mission lands.

Pope Paul VI took up this idea in 1975 in his apostolic exhortation *Evangelii Nuntiandi* about evangelization in the modern world, and Pope John Paul II often spoke with urgency about the task of a second, new evangelization of Europe. In this situation, Christianity is taking on a new historical form today, and we are only at the beginning of this new beginning. These words are, of course, open to misunderstanding. In every century, the church is the same; but she is always *en route* to the discovery of the inexhaustible newness of the gospel. The Second Vatican Council gave the directions for this in good time, and its teachings are a reliable compass for the path that the church must take in the twenty-first century.

Unfortunately, not everyone has yet grasped the full extent of the upheaval, the challenge, and the necessary new missionary orientation of pastoral work. Many stay where they are, intent on consolidating what they have; many are afraid of anything new. Many want to go on, as far as possible, in the style to which they are accustomed, but this will not be possible in the long term. If we are to cross what John Paul II called the "threshold of hope," a rethinking and a reorientation are needed. Structural changes too will be necessary, but these tend to get bogged down unless the new beginning is above all a spiritual exodus. This affects all the members of the church, and in a particular manner the self-understanding and ministry of the priest. "It is the Spirit who makes alive" (John 6:63). Without him, as the Sequence at Mass on Pentecost Sunday says, there is "nothing good in deed or thought, nothing free from taint of ill."

Looking Back in Gratitude

If the exodus is not to be a mere aimless wandering, we must know both the landscape and our goal. This presupposes retrospection, for only when we look back do we see where we stand today, and what our point of departure is. I should like to look back from the perspective of my own personal experience of life as a priest in the past fifty years.

Fifty years ago, I would never even have dreamed that I would one day spend the last period of my ministry in Rome. At that time, I had one simple and perfectly normal wish: I wanted to become a parish priest. This idea was kindled in me at a very early age in the atmosphere and education I received in our family, where religion was taken for granted as a central element. Family prayer in common was a matter of course. One of my earliest childhood memories is of sitting in the organ loft alongside my father, who was a teacher and who conducted the church choir. When the Third Reich put a stop to religious education in schools, my mother taught us with the aid of religious textbooks belonging to my father, who, like almost all the young men, had been drafted into the army. This religious world decisively rejected the ideology of the Third Reich. We were proud that our bishop, Johannes Baptista Sproll, spoke out courageously in public against the Nazis, especially on the occasion of episcopal visitations; for us, he was the "confessor bishop." This spirit of resistance, born of faith, inevitably strengthened my desire to become a priest.

My definitive decision was taken when I was in high school in the first decade after the war. In this period, there was a fresh blossoming of the youth movement, which had done so much between the wars to prepare the way for the subsequent renewal of the church. I met some fine young priests to whom I remain abidingly grateful, since they influenced me for life. They introduced me at an early age to the spirit of the liturgical movement and the biblical movement. To mention only two: Franz Lenk, the rector of the seminary, and Anton Herre, later auxiliary bishop in Rottenburg, who remained a fatherly friend and mentor until the first years of my own ministry as bishop.

Those postwar years were very different from today's situation. After the Nazi period and the total collapse in 1945, church life flourished anew—though only briefly. The biblical movement, the liturgical movement, and the first phase of the ecumenical movement laid the foundations for the breakthrough in the 1960s at the Second Vatican Council. Even during my time as a curate in Stuttgart at the close of the 1950s, however, it was perfectly obvious that a process of disintegration and crisis was beginning, especially in pastoral work among the young. Contrary to what many people think, the upheaval began long before the council.

We who were young priests at that time experienced the Second Vatican Council in a way that is scarcely conceivable today: as a radically new beginning, the work of the Holy Spirit. The period of the council and the immediate postconciliar years made a very deep impression on us, which has lasted up to the present day. For despite all the signs of crisis that were visible even then, the biblical, liturgical, and pastoral renewal bore good fruit in those years. But then came the cultural upheaval of 1968 and the early 1970s, bringing a new wave of secularization and a frosty period of contestation in the church. Postconciliar enthusiasm expected great things, but in fact, many aspects of ecclesial life took a decided turn for the worse: fewer people attended Mass, and the numbers of baptisms, church weddings, and confessions declined, as did the number of seminarians and novices in religious life. Many priests and religious gave up their ministries, and this too was a severe blow to the vitality of the church.

In those difficult years, I owed much to the confidence shown by the two bishops of our diocese, first to Bishop Carl Joseph Leipreicht, who ordained me to the priesthood in Rottenburg in 1957, and then to Bishop Georg Moser, my immediate predecessor. I am grateful likewise to Cardinal Joseph Höffner, whom I met during my time in Münster, to Cardinal Hermann Volk, and to Cardinal Julius Doepfner. During the Second Vatican Council and the difficult years of upheaval that followed it, these three cardinals were outstanding leaders who provided orientation and a point of reference for many people.

In recent times, thank God, we see positive signs of new spiritual beginnings in parishes, religious orders, and spiritual movements. People are asking once again about God and about the fundamental values that make life possible; one might say that it has once more become "respectable" to ask religious questions. Much of what is called spirituality today may indeed be cloudy and immature, and much may also be profoundly ambivalent. To borrow Romano Guardini's phrase, the "discernment of what is Christian" is needed here. Nevertheless, we may indeed hope that the prophecy of Pope John XXIII about a new Pentecost will be fulfilled, and that the little plants emerging from the soil in a new spring will one day bear a rich harvest.

In my own case, those years were spent in academic work, and I look back on my three decades in the university world with pleasure and gratitude. The intellectual climate of those years was exceptionally stimulating and lively. When I was a young professor in Münster, my colleagues included Karl Rahner, Joseph Ratzinger, and Johann Baptist Metz. At Tübingen, they included Alfons Auer, Hans Küng, and Max Seckler; and the contact and dialogue with my Protestant colleagues in that city, Jürgen Moltmann and Eberhard Jüngel, were friendly and fruitful. We spent long evenings discussing every theological subject under the sun—"God and the world," as we say in German.

Naturally, church debates soon made an impact on the theological faculties too, where they sometimes led to strife and dissensions. People had to declare where they stood, and polarizations resulted. This made the atmosphere harsh and difficult. Nevertheless, I have positive memories of my conversations with the students, which were often critical but always stimulating. I miss those conversations today. Questions about the training of future priests led me to reflect often and deeply about the priestly ministry. Since the priest ought to be a theologian, in the original sense of this word—that is, one who speaks about God and about our life in God—I have always understood my theological existence as a part of my priestly existence. And I have always regarded the homily as the touchstone of theology.

In my books *Einführung in den Glauben* (1972; English: *An Introduction to Christian Faith*), *Jesus der Christus* (1974; English: *Jesus the Christ*), and *Der Gott Jesu Christi* (1982; English: *The God of Jesus Christ*), which have been translated into many languages, I attempted to make a contribution to the deepening of faith and to provide a helpful orientation in the central and fundamental issues. During my academic career, I shared on a regular basis in pastoral work in parishes, among students, and in hospital clinics, and I gained considerable pastoral experience above all through celebrating Mass and visiting patients in the Tübingen university clinics.

I also gained valuable experiences on my journeys abroad, especially through a semester as visiting professor in the United States, visits to Rome and Jerusalem to hold guest lectures, and my first journeys to Africa and Asia. Lectures and friendly encounters with professors in East Berlin, in the then-communist East Germany, and in other countries behind the Iron Curtain, especially Poland and the Czech Republic, were very important too. They showed me that we could not simply take for granted our Western situation, where the church can carry out her ministry in peace and freedom, and where she has a good financial basis. This is not at all the normal situation for the church.

After 1989, the year in which the Berlin Wall came down, I had ten years of intensive pastoral experience as the bishop of a large diocese that was pluriform both sociologically and in terms of religious denominations. Rottenburg-Stuttgart was truly alive, but also challenging. We could not hide our heads in the sand to avoid seeing the upheavals and the need for new pastoral orientations, but all we had were early pointers to answers. These were far from mature; so consensus was a long way off. During these years, I had many conversations with priests who carried out their ministry with confidence and joy—and with other priests who were in the process of giving up their ministry. I still vividly recall many of these conversations, which significantly broadened my own priestly experience. I remember with special pleasure my pastoral visits to the parishes, which took place nearly every Sunday, and the ordinations of deacons and priests, which were always attended by large numbers of the people of God. This was a clear testimony to the fact that the people of God need and want priests, pray for priests, and are grateful for priests.

I remember with gratitude the collegial and friendly cooperation in the ecclesiastical province of Freiburg in southwest Germany with Archbishop Oscar Saier and Bishop Karl Lehmann. We were able to share our good (and our less good) pastoral experiences with one another in an attitude of great openness and mutual trust; we discussed the problems in the church and gave one another support. This was genuine collegiality, both affective and effective, as intended by the council. My collaboration with the bishops of the local Protestant church, Theo

Sorg and his successor, Eberhardt Renz, was always marked by openness, trust, and friendship.

Among my many activities as diocesan bishop were visits to many countries in the so-called Third World, where I encountered non-European pastoral realities, especially situations of poverty and misery. Many of these journeys moved me deeply, and I returned to Germany a changed man. From then on, I have been convinced that while Europe has abiding significance for the worldwide church, we must avoid making our European problems and points of view the only valid criterion. In old Europe, we can learn from the young churches not only how to be young but also how to draw new confidence from our faith. Since that time, I have attached great importance to dialogue and exchange between the various cultures.

The last eight years have brought a completely unexpected new phase in my life. This period in the Eternal City has enriched me with worldwide ecumenical experiences in East and West as well as in the Southern Hemisphere, and with numerous friendly meetings with the bishops, theologians, and pastors of other churches. Here, one can sense something of the blowing of the Holy Spirit, who urges us on toward unity; and this makes our perception of the pain and the scandal of separation all the more acute. I should also like to mention in gratitude the almost daily experience—enriching and nearly always pleasant—of the worldwide church. Its colorful variety does not in any way impair its union with the successor of Peter. These years have seen meetings and exchanges of views with innumerable bishops, priests, laypersons, students, theologians, ambassadors, and journalists from every country in the world. And I recall with particular gratitude my regular meetings with John Paul II and Benedict XVI. Both these popes have seen the discussion of ecumenical questions as an expression of their apostolic "concern for all the churches" (2 Cor 11:28).

Docta Spes—Looking Ahead in Hope

The fifty years of my priestly ministry move me to tremendous gratitude and inspire me to look to the future with hope. We cannot deny that the church has many problems and that she suffers great oppression in several countries. At the same time, however, the words of Benedict XVI in his first sermon as pope are true: the church is alive, she is young, dynamic, and vital. This is how I too would sum up my experiences over the past fifty years.

Others have traveled along different roads, and their experiences are different; this is why I would not wish to generalize my own. In any case, subjective personal impressions and experiences cannot be a reliable criterion and a sure foundation on which to construct one's life, one's own future, or the future of the church. Hope needs a more reliable foundation, and this has been laid once and for all in Jesus Christ (1 Cor 3:11).

Accordingly, I will leave my personal experiences in the background in the following chapters and take as my criterion the original biblical testimony, in a spiritual reading of the New Testament. This gives us the universally applicable criterion. In the New Testament, we meet the testimony of the experiences of the first Christians, the first communities, disciples, and apostles. This testimony remains the model and the typological criterion for every subsequent generation. It bears witness to the explosive beginnings of the Christian mission, which can inspire us and stimulate us today.

It would, of course, be naïve to think that we could simply block out the developments of later centuries and leap back directly into the first century. One can compare the original testimony to an inexhaustible spring from which fresh water bubbles up; in the course of tradition, this has grown into a mighty river. We cannot reverse the course it has taken, but fresh, pure water must continually flow into it from its origin, for otherwise this river will turn into a stagnant pond or else overflow its banks and mingle with other streams. It is in this sense that we can draw on the original testimony to refresh and renew ecclesial life. Our task today is not to reinvent the priesthood, but to let ourselves be renewed by the power of the origin and to set out with fresh vigor on the path that lies ahead.

The New Testament can give us inspiration and input for our new beginning. Input, however, is not a straightforward recipe. Scripture does not and indeed cannot give

One can compare the original testimony to an inexhaustible spring from which fresh water bubbles up; in the course of tradition, this has grown into a mighty river. We cannot reverse the course it has taken, but fresh, pure water must continually flow into it from its origin. We can draw on the original testimony to refresh and renew ecclesial life.

us recipes for our life; rather, it invites us to a new way of thinking and to a conscientious examination of what is right before God. This invitation presupposes that we are willing to rethink our position and to let ourselves be renewed. The apostle Paul calls this kind of reflection, which is willing to learn and to change one's life, "worship with one's mind" (Rom 12:1f.).

This is why the path ahead is not a frivolous adventure. The church has always maintained the principle of *fides quaerens intellectum*, the faith that seeks to understand. The same is true of hope: it will often be a "hope against hope" (Rom 4:18), but it also wishes to be a *docta spes*, an "instructed hope." As Christians, we are called to give an account (*apologia* in Greek) of the hope that is in us (1 Pet 3:15). We ought to be able to say what we hope for and why we hope; why we live as priests, and what the purpose of our priestly life is. This cannot be done without theological reflection.

A hopeful look to the future is not the work of a naïve youthful enthusiasm—especially after fifty years' experience! The Christian hope is different from a purely human optimism. It is neither a happy human quality nor an ephemeral mood. Rather, it is based on the substance of the gospel, on the cross and resurrection of Jesus Christ.

This hope, rooted in the paschal mystery, convinces me that the priesthood has a future, despite and in the midst of all the difficulties. Creative forms of vocational pastoral work can play a useful role here; above all, it is vital to speak personally to young men about the possibility that God is calling them to this ministry, and then to accompany them on their spiritual journey, since the most convincing form of vocational pastoral work takes place when young men meet priests who reflect the splendor of the truth of the faith (*veritatis splendor*) and its inherent beauty, and who bear witness to this with confidence and joy. Here, it is helpful to reflect on the ministry and spirituality of the priest, for ultimately it is only the splendor of the truth that can make the priestly ministry attractive and radiant.

On the basis of this conviction, I can repeat the words that stood on the prayer card marking my ordination and first Mass fifty years ago: in the future, just as in the past, the priest will be a "servant of joy" (2 Cor 1:4).

2

Priestly Existence— Christian Existence

Personal Friendship with Christ

While I was still in high school, I read Romano Guardini's well-known book *The Lord,* and I realized that the heart of the Christian faith is not an idea or a pastoral strategy, still less an ideology. The heart of the Christian faith is a person, Jesus Christ. He says of himself: "I am the way, the truth, and the life" (John 14:8). We find many such "I am . . ." statements in the Fourth Gospel (4:26; 6:48; 8:12, etc.), and they correspond to some extent to the summons to follow Jesus in the Synoptic Gospels: "Follow me!" (Mark 1:17, etc.), which means: "Come and live with me and learn from me." Before Jesus sent his disciples out, they were to be with him (Mark 3:14), sharing his life and living with him (John 1:38f.), pupils in his school, so to speak—a school of life, and later on, a school of suffering.

The Gospel of John puts this even more beautifully when it quotes the words of Jesus: "No longer do I call you servants, for the servant does not know what his master is doing; but I have called you friends, for all that I have heard from my Father I have made known to you" (15:15). Like Christian existence in general, priestly existence can be grasped, lived, and attested only on the basis of a personal friendship with Jesus Christ that is practiced and continually renewed and deepened. If we are to understand Jesus, we must lean on his breast like the beloved disciple John at the Last Supper (John 13:23). There is a famous sculpture depicting this scene, the *Johannesminne* ("John's love"), in the former convent of Cistercian nuns, now a center for Christian seminars and courses, at Heiligkreuztal in Upper Swabia in our diocese. This work of art has always moved me, and I have often meditated on its message.

The present situation of indifference vis-à-vis God and of the apparent absence and silence of God is a particularly urgent invitation to reflection. We very frequently encounter the questions: "Where is God? Why is he not here? Where does he show himself?" But "no one has ever seen God; the only Son, who is in the bosom of the Father, he has made him known" (John 1:18). This is why he can say: "Whoever has seen me has seen the Father" (14:9). In him, the incarnate Son of God, the invisible God, has become visible on a human face. Accordingly, friendship and fellowship with Jesus mean fellowship and friendship with God and fellowship and friendship with one another, life and perfect joy (1 John 1:1-4).

Friendship with Jesus Christ is the answer to the ultimate and deepest question we human beings have, the question about life and about the happy life that we can have only in God. It is friendship with Jesus—indeed, passion for him and for his "cause," the kingdom of God as a kingdom of life, of justice, of holiness, and of peace—that makes the priest a "theologian" in the original sense of the word, that is, one who can speak about the God who has a human face. Such a priest can therefore give an answer to the deepest existential human questions not only with his speech but with his entire existence. In this way he can bring light, life, and joy into the darkness that reigns in many people's lives. And it is in this way that he can be a "servant of joy" (2 Cor 1:24).

The Christological Reinterpretation of the Priesthood

Readers familiar with the contemporary debates in biblical theology may be surprised to see that I take Jesus Christ as my starting point; for in the wake of the crisis that has spread since the profound cultural upheavals and ruptures of the late 1960s and early 1970s, it has often been emphasized that Jesus never described himself as a priest; and scholars have tended rather to place Jesus in the tradition of the prophets who criticized the Temple cult. Jesus claimed of himself: "Here is one who is greater than the Temple" (Matt 12:6). Like the prophets, he sharply criticized the cultic practice of his time. The cleansing of the Temple is the most dramatic expression of this critique (Mark 11:15-19). Jesus' words about demolishing and rebuilding the Temple played an important role in his trial (Mark 14:58), and it was the conflict with the priestly aristocracy of his days, the Sadducees, that ultimately led to Jesus' condemnation and execution.

Some theologians have regarded these observations as a solid biblical argument that allows them to overthrow the special priesthood of the new covenant. But while these observations are not false, they are only half of the truth. Even in the prophets of the Old Testament we find a constructive reinterpretation of priesthood and sacrifice alongside their harsh critique of the contemporary priestly caste and sacrificial cult. Something similar can be said of Jesus: his critique of the contemporary Temple cult is linked to a new understanding of priesthood.

We find this reinterpretation most clearly in the Songs of the Servant of Yahweh in Second Isaiah, especially in the fourth song (53:1-12), which speaks of the Servant of God who has borne our sicknesses and let himself be burdened with our pains. He was pierced for our transgressions and crushed because of our sins; through his wounds we have been healed. The Lord laid on him the guilt of us all. The song closes by speaking of his vicarious suffering and dying "for many." This is described as an expiatory sacrifice through which the Servant, who is righteous, makes many persons righteous (verses 10-12). These affirmations (which are often quoted in the New Testament) take up the traditional cultic language but give it a new meaning—deeper, personal, spiritual.

We find a similar reinterpretation in the Psalms: for example, "For you have no delight in sacrifice; if I were to give a burnt offering, you would not be pleased. The sacrifice acceptable to God is a broken spirit; a broken and contrite heart, O God, you will not despise" (51:18f.). The Psalms also speak of the "sacrifice of praise" (50:14, 23). Some scholars have called this personal reinterpretation a "spiritualization" of the traditional ideas about cultic sacrifice, but this misses the point, since the offering of the human heart in the fourth Servant Song and in the Psalms has not only an internal dimension. It also has a concrete, bodily aspect: "You have given me an open ear. . . . I delight to do your will, O God" (Ps 40:7-9).

Jesus takes up this reinterpretation of the ideas of sacrifice and priesthood. A typical expression of his own self-understanding is the statement that he has come "to give his life as a ransom for many" (Mark 10:45 par.). The theology of the Servant of Yahweh sees priestly existence as a vicarious action on behalf of those who deserve death because of their sin. This is not understood in the sense of a "replacement" of these persons, which would exclude them from action, but rather in the sense of a "pro-existence," a life which is lived and laid down "for many" in order that they may have life.

The unsurpassable form that this existence takes on our behalf is revealed during the last meal that Jesus held with his disciples on the evening before his passion and death. The Last Supper is a summary of his entire life; it is also the anticipation of his suffering and of his resurrection. In the version of the words of institution that we find in Mark and Matthew, Jesus speaks at the Last Supper of the "blood of the covenant" (Mark 14:24; Matt 26:28). Here, he alludes to the covenant sacrifice offered by Moses on Mount Sinai (Exod 24:8)—in other words, Jesus is using the priestly sacrificial terminology. In the version that we find in Paul and Luke, Jesus has recourse to the prophetic tradition (Jer 31:31) and speaks of the "new covenant" (Luke 22:20; 1 Cor 11:25) and of the gift of himself "for the many" (Isa 53:12). Here, the cultic and hieratic ideas of sacrifice are interpreted prophetically as the personal sacrifice of his own self. In other words, Jesus does not wish to sacrifice some *thing* to God. He sacrifices himself. His whole existence is a radical existence for God and for us.

The Fourth Gospel grasped the profound significance of this reinterpretation. Jesus' farewell discourses in John are preceded by these words: "Having loved his own who were in the world, he loved them to the end" (13:1). In the farewell discourses, Jesus calls this love, which goes to the uttermost end, the love of friends: "You are my friends. . . . No one has greater love than this, to lay down one's life for one's friends" (15:13). The First Letter of John echoes these words: "We know love by this, that he laid down his life for us" (3:16). Jesus' priesthood is thus a friendship that goes to the uttermost end and has only one goal: "that your joy may be complete" (John 15:11; cf. 16:24; 1 John 1:4; 2 John 12).

We also find this reinterpretation in the Letter to the Hebrews, which presents a more detailed discussion of Jesus' priesthood than any other New Testament writing. The central point of reference is Psalm 110, which plays an important role in the synoptic tradition about Jesus (Mark 12:35f.; 14:16f. par.) and in the post-Easter christology (Acts 2:34). The Letter to the Hebrews quotes the verse "You are a priest forever according to the order of Melchizedek" (Ps 110:4), which refers to the mysterious figure of the pagan high priest Melchizedek (Gen 14:18-20). Hebrews affirms that Jesus is a priest according to the order of Melchizedek and that he is the eschatological fulfillment of this priesthood. The letter interprets Jesus' sacrifice in the prophetic tradition, as a self-sacrifice (Heb 7:27), and puts the following words from Psalm 40:7-9 on Jesus' lips when he comes into the world: "Sacrifices and offerings you have not desired, but a body you have prepared for me; in burnt offerings and sin offerings you have taken no pleasure. Then I said, 'See, God, I have come to do your will, O God (in the scroll of the book it is written of me)'" (Heb 10:5-7).

According to Hebrews, therefore, both the cultic understanding of priesthood and sacrifice in pagan religions (represented by Melchizedek) and the understanding found in the Old Testament (represented by the levitical priesthood) are annulled through the work of Jesus. At the same time, however, they are raised to a higher level. By his death on the cross, Jesus both perfects and terminates all human priesthood (Heb 7:27; 9:1; 10:10). He is the definitive and true high priest, the mediator of the new covenant (Heb 8:6, 13; 9:15; 12:24). He is the one and only mediator between God and humankind (I Tim 2:5).

The objection mentioned above is correct when it points out that Jesus was not a member of the priestly caste at that time. His self-understanding was not modeled on the priests in the Jerusalem Temple, and he did not see himself as a cultic official. But Jesus Christ is the priest of the new covenant in a qualitatively new and deeper sense. He does not offer God some *thing* in sacrifice; he offers his own self in sacrifice, and he does this as the ultimate and highest possible service of friendship for us. In our situation, in thrall to sin and hence to death (Rom 5:12), we are incapable of helping ourselves, still less of saving ourselves: Jesus takes our place and gives us new life through this vicarious service of friendship.

Understood in this way, the priesthood of Jesus belongs to the center and heart of the Christian faith. It is the revelation of the deepest mystery of God, for God is love (I John 4:8, 16). "God so loved the world that he gave his only Son, so that everyone who believes in him may not perish but may have eternal life" (John 3:16). This love that gives itself for us is the foundation on which the whole of the Christian life is built. The mystery of this love is an inexhaustible subject of meditation. We can ponder it again and again, giving thanks with all our heart.

The Common Priesthood of All Christians

With his priestly existence, Jesus is the model and archetype not only of the priest but of every Christian. It was above all the council that reopened the path to the insight into the common priesthood of all Christians—an insight that removed many a priest from his lofty pedestal. This insight, however, was wrongly understood as putting a question mark against the special ordained priesthood. It never attached a "higher" value to the laity in order to "devalue" the priest; on the contrary, it also enriched the self-understanding of the priest and revealed to him in a new way his true dignity within the whole people of God. Above all, this insight showed us that a good priest must first of all be a good Christian. Here, he is no different from anyone else. One can only be a priest together with everyone else, not on some separate level. All Christian existence is priestly existence, and priestly existence must first and foremost be a Christian existence.

But it is here that the real problem begins. For what is a Christian existence? What does it mean to be a Christian? It is impossible to give an adequate answer in a few words, but Jesus summarized the essential point in the principal commandment to love God with all one's heart and above all else, and to love one's neighbor as oneself (Mark 12:29-31). This primary and most important commandment, which is the synthesis of every other precept (Rom 13:9), is linked directly to the message that God is love and that he loved us first. On the basis of his service of friendship for us, Jesus draws the following conclusion in the Fourth Gospel: "Love one another as I have loved you" (John 15:12). And we find the same conclusion in the First Letter of John: "We too ought to lay down our lives for our brothers and sisters" (3:16).

The principal commandment tells us that we must let ourselves be seized by the love of God in Jesus Christ, making this completely our own in order to be wholly the friend of God and wholly the friend of our fellow human beings and the servant of joy. In his great hymn to love, Paul tells us what this love is. It exceeds even the greatest prophetic and charismatic gifts, since these are only fragmentary and will one day cease. But love abides forever (1 Cor 13).

Christian existence is thus an *ex-sistere*, a going out of oneself and beyond oneself. Unlike the sin, which is in love with itself, it seeks not itself, but the other. Its point of reference lies not in itself, but in the other; the pull of gravity is not toward itself, but toward him or her, and above all towards *the* Other, namely, God. Christian existence overcomes and forgets egocentricity. In an act of self-transcendence, it moves toward God and other people. Its concern is the greater glory of God, as Saint Ignatius of Loyola said, and thus it imitates God's movement of love toward human beings. A love of this kind drives out fear (I John 4:18). In boundless trust, it sheds the existential fear that lives within us, knowing that it is safe in God in every situation, since nothing—neither oppression, persecution, distress, or death—can separate us from the love of God (Rom 8:35, 39).

In this double movement of love for God and for our neighbor, the Christian existence imitates Jesus. It accepts the idea of vicarious action on behalf of another. It does not value its own importance too highly, and it is ready to make space for others. It is willing to bear others' burdens in a spirit of solidarity (Gal 6:2). This may at first sight seem an excessive burden, but Jesus is aware of the inherent dialectic of such a love: he tells us that the one who loses his life will win it (Mark 8:35 par.); happiness and bliss are not to be found in self-seeking but in giving away one's own self. One finds joy by creating joy. This makes the Christian existence essentially a priestly existence. It is no longer possible to understand it as a question of the salvation of the individual; it is a missionary existence for others.

The apostle Paul sees the Christian existence as essentially based on baptism. In his exhortation about baptism in Romans 6, he explains that this sacrament means dying with Christ, in order to be dead to sin and to live in Christ for God, totally and forever; and this is how he defines Christian freedom in another passage. He begins with a lapidary formulation: "For freedom Christ has set us free." But he knows that the great word "freedom" can be seductive, and this is why he goes on: "You were called to freedom, brothers and sisters; only do not use your freedom as an opportunity for self-indulgence, but through love become slaves to one another" (Gal 5:1, 13; cf. 1 Pet 2:16).

Christian freedom would be misunderstood if it were to be thought of in terms of self-seeking and arbitrary conduct. It is realized in selfless love (a word that must, of course, be understood in the correct sense). Christian freedom is freedom from the slavery of egoistic ties; it is free from itself and therefore free for others. As Martin Luther once said, Christian freedom makes one the free sovereign over everything, and thus also the servant of everyone.

In another context, Paul speaks of freedom in love as a sacrifice, and this means that this freedom is a basic priestly attitude. Paul speaks of offering one's life and of the sacrifice and worship of the faith of the community (Phil 2:17). He writes that the entire community should become a sacrificial gift that pleases God (Rom 15:16). This theology of sacrifice and this kind of sacrificial existence may strike us as strange and joyless, but Paul thought differently. He would have regarded a joyless Christianity as no Christianity at all, and a sad Christian as a very poor sort of Christian, since it is only when we break out of the narrowness of our own self that we discover the richness of life in the encounter with others, and *a fortiori* in the encounter with God. This is why the kingdom of God is joy in the Holy Spirit (Rom 14:17), and the apostle never tires of telling his readers, "Rejoice in the Lord always; again I will say, Rejoice!" (Phil 4:4; cf. 3:1).

All these affirmations about the essence of the Christian existence are necessary if we are to understand why the First Letter of Peter speaks of the people of God as a priestly people and a royal priesthood (2:5, 9; cf. Rev 1:6; 5:10; 20:6). This text has rightly been regarded as the fundamental text for the doctrine of the common priesthood of all Christians; but it must be read in the light of both the Old Testament (Exod 19; Isa 61:6) and the New. Read in this way, it provides no support (as is often wrongly asserted) for a quasi-democratic participation by the laity in the government of the church. The text is concerned with something much more basic than a share in decision making. It is a fundamental affirmation that we are all Christians and all make up the church.

The First Letter of Peter speaks of the construction of a spiritual house that is made up of living stones and rests on the cornerstone, Jesus Christ, who is chosen by God. It calls this spiritual building of living stones "holy" and a "royal priesthood"; "holy" because it is separated from the other peoples and belongs to God in a special way, and "royal" because it enjoys kingly freedom and self-determination, and is not subject to any coercion. This royal freedom is not, however, understood as an arbitrary freedom of the will, but as a priestly service "to offer through Jesus Christ spiritual sacrifices which are pleasing to God." The foundation and criterion of the royal priesthood of all Christians are thus not our own will but Jesus Christ and his priestly service for us. He is the cornerstone who bears everything and binds it all together. He is the criterion and the point of orientation.

A priestly existence of this kind is not restricted to a priestly class or caste. This royal and priestly dignity is the distinguishing mark of all who follow Jesus, and imposes an obligation on them. All are brothers and sisters; and all are friends (3 John 15). This too seems to have been a self-designation of the early Christians. The special priestly ministry is based on this common priestly existence of all Christians, which has its roots in baptism. As we shall see shortly, it cannot be derived from the common priestly existence of all, but it shares in this. Accordingly, before a priest can be sent out to his own specific form of service, he must first grow with all the

The foundation and criterion of the royal priesthood of all Christians are thus not our own will but Jesus Christ and his priestly service for us. He is the cornerstone who bears everything and binds it all together. He is the criterion and the point of orientation.

tle ones, and the powerless (Matt 5:3-10; Luke 6:20-22). She praises the God who does great things for us and has mercy from generation to generation, the God who casts down the arrogant and powerful from their thrones and takes care of the lowly, the God who is faithful to the promises that he made to our ancestors. Mary, the first disciple, is also the first witness to the good news of the gospel.

This is why Luke's infancy narrative is completely permeated by the climate of joy that comes from this good news. The angel says to Mary, "Rejoice (*chaire*)!" (Luke 1:28), and as soon as she sets out to visit her cousin Elizabeth, she becomes the messenger who communicates this joy. When he encounters Mary (who bears Jesus in her womb), John (who will become the Baptist and forerunner of Jesus) leaps for joy in the womb of his mother, Elizabeth (1:41, 44). Both Mary's song of praise in the *Magnificat* and Zechariah's song of praise in the *Benedictus* express the joy that God has visited his people and redeemed them (1:68). At the birth of Jesus, the angels announce "great joy for all the people" (2:10). This same joy overflows onto Simeon and the prophetess Anna, who have not abandoned hope even in their old age (2:29–32, 38).

Mary remained faithful to her vocation to the bitter end, when she stood under the cross of her Son. At the end, the messenger of joy becomes the mother of sorrows, but she *stood* under the cross (*Stabat mater*), while the other disciples, apart from John, fled. Steadfast in love, she united herself to the sacrifice of her Son. This is why the crucified Jesus made Mary the mother of John, the disciple whom he especially loved (John 19:26f.). For the Fourth Gospel, John is the typological representative of discipleship, and this means that in him, we have all received Mary as our mother. Each one us individually, like the church as a whole, is entrusted to her motherly care and protection.

Accordingly, we see Mary with the disciples and the women who had followed Jesus, united in prayer for the coming of the Spirit between the ascension of Jesus and the day of Pentecost (Acts 1:14). She herself was over-shadowed by the Holy Spirit, who filled her completely (Luke 1:35), and now she is with the church when we pray for renewal through the same Spirit. She prays today for a new Pentecost and gives her motherly support to the renewal of the church through the Holy Spirit. Thus it is not by chance that all the spiritual beginnings in the church in recent years, especially the spiritual movements, have a clearly Marian character.

With only a little exaggeration, we can say that Mary is not only Catholic—she is also, indeed primarily, "evangelical" in the real sense of the word. She is a woman of the gospel, a woman to whom the gospel bears witness, and many Protestant Christians are discovering Mary for the first time today. According to the gospel, she played a unique role in the history of our salvation. As the

mother of Jesus, she is the mother of the Lord (*kyrios,*
Luke 1:43), and all Christendom calls her *theotokos,* the
"Mother of God"—a title confirmed by the Third Ecumenical Council in 431. She is also our mother, mother
of Christians and mother of the church. As Hans Urs
von Balthasar wrote, she represents the charismatic
dimension, which is a constituent element in the life of
the church alongside the institutional, "Petrine" dimension.

Mary preserved and pondered in her heart everything
that she had seen (Luke 2:19, 51). In the same way, the
church later preserved spiritually, pondered, and unfolded
the scriptural testimony to the mother of Jesus. In this
spiritual reading of the Bible, innumerable priests have
seen her as the archetype of the church and of discipleship, and she has become their mother and intercessor in
all their personal and pastoral needs. This is why a
"healthy" Marian piety should always have its place in the
life of a priest. I, at any rate, cannot imagine things differently. I am convinced that Mary is united to us today
through her powerful intercession as we all pray for a
renewed Pentecost, which will be a springtime for the
church. And I am convinced that every priest receives her
motherly care.

3

The Priest
in His Apostolic Mission

Jesus Calls His First Disciples

In the years after the Second Vatican Council, the distinction and relationship between priests and laity has frequently been a problem in many places. If we read scripture, we soon observe that Jesus chose a number of men, mentioned by name, out of the larger group of his disciples. He called these men to follow him more closely and then sent them out in a special way. All four Gospels agree on this point (Mark 1:16-20 par.; 3:13-19 par.; John 1:35-51).

Each of these texts repays detailed reflection. For example, the Fourth Gospel transmits a very personal account of the calling of the first disciples (John 1:35-

51), the story of an initially shy friendship with Jesus that leads into a permanent sharing of his life. Many vocations even today take the same course. The first disciples remembered the exact hour of the day at which Jesus had called them—"it was about the tenth hour" (John 1:39)—and I myself recall a sermon that I heard when I was in high school. It gripped me so profoundly that I can still quote some of the preacher's words.

I will draw on Mark 3:13-19 for my theological exposition of the call of the disciples; this passage has meant a great deal to me since my seminary days. It tells us that so many people were present that Jesus withdrew to a mountain, as he always did when he had to make important decisions. Here, "he called to him those whom he wanted." The vocation to a special form of discipleship is thus a sovereign act of the free divine choice. This does not obliterate the freedom of those who are called in this manner, since they must *follow* the call. And so we read: "And they came to him." They accept the call and follow Jesus. This is a radical decision. Another passage tells us that they leave everything behind them—house, family, and employment (Mark 1:18; 10:28 par.).

Despite the radical character of the disciples' decision, the central reality is not this decision itself, since the disciples do not make themselves disciples! Rather, the invitation that is addressed to them is a word of power. Mark writes: "he *made* [*epoiēsen* in Greek] the twelve," that is, *he* made them his disciples. His call is a creative word that brings about what it says, making disciples of those whom he calls. This is another indication of the absolute newness and the creative quality of the special vocation to discipleship.

When he calls them, he defines the two goals of their discipleship: they are to be with Jesus and in his fellowship, and then they are to be sent out. Assembly and mission— or contemplation and action—are indissolubly linked. The exercise of mission is not an impersonal function that one assumes for a time; it leaves its imprint on the entire existence, and a total mission of this kind, which involves the entire personality, can be lived and undertaken only on the basis of personal fellowship with Jesus.

A final point: the disciples who are called and sent out are mentioned individually by name. They are not anonymous, interchangeable, impersonal functionaries; they have a name, and this means that they are known and acknowledged as men who commit their whole person to their "cause." They are witnesses who testify to their words with their whole person. And it is only as witnesses of this kind that they are convincing. Only in this way can they be "fishers of men" who win people over (Mark 1:17).

The first name in the lists of the apostles is always Simon, to whom Jesus gives the new name Cephas/Peter (Mark 3:16; John 1:40-44). In the Bible, the bestowal of a name is never a mere change of "label." It always has a deeper meaning, expressing a new qualification, a new function, and a new position. During Jesus' earthly ministry, Peter was already the spokesman and representative of the group of disciples; he was also the first witness to the resurrection (Luke 24:34; I Cor 15:5). He was to be the "rock" (*petra* in Greek) on which the church is built (Matt 16:18; see John 21:15-17), and it would be his task to strengthen his brethren (Luke 22:32).

These passages that speak of a special commission entrusted to Simon Peter were very influential even in the New Testament period, and their importance has increased throughout the history of the church; we cannot go into the details here. Instead, let us look briefly at the moving human figure of Peter, this "rock man" who was no hero or superman, but a weak man who made mistakes, which are not glossed over or toned down in the New Testament, because the New Testament knows no personality cults. Even in his weaknesses, Peter shows us something about discipleship: Jesus does not demand a superhuman heroism from his disciples. No one is to boast, because our power does not come from our own selves. On the contrary, the power of Christ is made manifest *in* our weakness. But at the same time, the disciples of Jesus can rely on the assurance that Paul received: "My grace is enough for you" (2 Cor 12:9).

On the Foundation of the Apostles

The noun *apostolos* ("apostle") is not employed by Mark when he tells us how Jesus sent out the twelve (Mark 6:6-

12 par.); he uses only the verb *apostellein,* "to send out." In the first two Synoptic Gospels, there are only a few isolated and probably secondary instances of the title "apostle" during the earthly ministry of Jesus (Mark 6:30; Matt 10:2). Luke uses it more frequently when he writes about this period (Luke 6:13; 17:5, etc.). When it became common at a later date to speak of "the twelve apostles," this was owing to the influence of the Lukan conception.

Behind the biblical understanding of apostleship lies the rabbinic institution of the *shaliach,* which is based on the principle that the one sent is equivalent to the one who sends him. This means that the emissary is not a mere servant or delegate: he represents the one who sends him. We hear an echo of this understanding in the New Testament: "Whoever listens to you listens to me, and whoever rejects you rejects me, and whoever rejects me rejects the one who sent me" (Luke 10:16; see Matt 10:40; John 13:20).

Ultimately, the mission of the apostles goes back to the mission that Jesus receives from the Father: "As the Father has sent me, so I send you" (John 20:21; see 17:18). Through the apostles, the eternal salvific mystery of God the Father, which has appeared in history in the concrete form of Jesus Christ, is to be revealed and made present among the peoples of the world (Eph 3:4-6, 9; Col 1:25-29), and this means that the apostles and the apostolic testimony belong constitutively to the mystery of revelation. It is only through them that this mystery can be grasped in history. And this is the foundation on which we stand (Eph 2:20).

We find differences on points of detail in the New Testament understanding of apostleship. Originally, as I have mentioned, we hear of "the twelve," not "the apostles." This means that they are chosen from the great crowd of disciples and appointed as representatives of the twelve tribes of the new people of Israel. They are not appointed as individuals, but as a community or (if one prefers the term) as a college. It is only in this way that they can be the representatives of the twelve tribes of Israel, the people that God has appointed to be a sign among the peoples of the world (Isa 11:12).

The appointment of the twelve thus signals both continuity and discontinuity with the twelve tribes of the people of Israel. All twelve belonged to the Jewish people whom God has chosen. As Paul was later to say, Israel is the root onto which the branch of the church was grafted and from which it can continue to derive nourishment (Rom 11:17). The church is a sign among the peoples; it is the shoot from the root of Israel which the prophets promised (Isa 11:10). This is why Paul sees peace between Jews and Gentiles and the sharing by the Gentiles in God's promises to Israel as fundamental and essential dimensions of the apostolic testimony (Eph 2:11-16; 3:6).

Subsequently, the salvation-historical link to the people of the old covenant was often forgotten or underestimated; it was only after the catastrophe of the Holocaust that it fully resurfaced in the consciousness of the church. In the light of the New Testament testimony, the new partnership that has come into being after the council between Jews—whom John Paul II called our "older brethren in the faith of Abraham"—and us Christians is one of the most important signs of a new beginning that will help us better to be a sign among the peoples. And in the aftermath of the tragic events of the twentieth century, this concerns us Germans in a special way.

In Luke's conception, there is not only a continuity with the people of the old covenant, but also a continuity between the activity of the earthly Jesus and the activity of the risen and exalted Lord. This is made clear in Luke's Acts of the Apostles, when Peter spells out the criteria for the election of a new apostle. The one to be elected (in this case Matthias) must be "one of the men who have accompanied us during all the time that the Lord Jesus went in and out among us, beginning from the baptism of John until the day that he was taken up from us—one of these must become a witness with us to his resurrection" (Acts 1:22f.; cf. 4:20; 10:38f.; 13:31).

Luke understands the apostles as eyewitnesses both of the earthly Jesus and of the risen Jesus who has been taken up into heaven. He considers it vitally important to preserve the continuity between the period of Jesus and the period of the church. Luke would decisively reject all the theories we hear today about a discontinuity between Jesus' activity and preaching on the one hand, and the church on the other, theories that often seek to appeal to the so-called historical Jesus in opposition to the church's message. There is no support anywhere in the New Testament for the slogan: "Jesus—yes; the church—no."

The emphasis in Paul is different, since he himself was not an eyewitness of the earthly Jesus. He came later; he calls himself "one untimely born" (I Cor 15:8). This is why he is not called an "apostle" in Acts but is regarded by Luke as an evangelist. Nevertheless, he understands himself as *the* apostle, who was called while in his mother's womb (Gal 1:15). He emphasizes that he was not called by human beings, but by Jesus Christ and by God himself (Gal 1:1). He sees the basis of his apostleship in the fact that he was counted worthy to be a direct witness of the risen Lord and to be sent out directly by Jesus (I Cor 9:1f.; Gal 1:15f.). He is conscious of being chosen and authorized to preach the gospel of God (Rom 1:1); he understands himself as the apostle of the Gentiles (Gal 1:7, 9; cf. Rom 1:5).

Naturally, Paul is not a loner who fights solitary battles. He is aware that he can carry out his ministry only in continuity and fellowship with the other apostles, and this is why he seeks acknowledgment by those who were apostles before him, especially Cephas and James—for otherwise, he might have "run in vain" (Gal 1:7-19). During his conflict with Cephas, he regards the reestablishing of fellowship with the other apostles as essential to the credibility and the enduring fruitfulness of his apostolic ministry (Gal 2:1-15; Acts 15).

In addition to the criterion of historical continuity, therefore, we have the criterion of community and collegiality. Both are anchored in the idea of the *communio* or *koinōnia*, the common participation in the life of the triune God (I John 1:3), which is fundamental for the church. This means that the apostolic ministry can be carried out only in a diachronic and synchronous fellowship. No individual can do everything on his own. Each one must take his place in the larger community and make the contribution of his own special charism. This is a basic argument against all sectarian schisms and exclusive claims—but also an argument against the complacent self-sufficiency of national and regional churches.

We find a summary of the apostolic foundation of the church in I Cor 15:3-9. This important text begins by quoting the ancient, traditional formulas that relate how the risen Jesus appeared to Cephas and the twelve. It then speaks of the apparition to more than five hundred brethren, to James, and to the other apostles. Finally, it speaks of the apparition to Paul. This summary is another indication of the plurality that was already present in the apostolic origins, but it also shows the common element: one is an apostle because of a direct encounter with the risen Lord, who directly sends one out as an authorized preacher of the gospel.

Thanks to their immediate encounter with the risen Lord and the mission that they received directly from him, the apostles belong constitutively to the original event whereby the church was founded. Our knowledge of the resurrection is not the knowledge of some neutral fact open to historical verification; we know about it only through the testimony of the apostles. Accordingly, they are the enduring foundation on which we stand, and they are our abiding point of reference (Eph 2:20). The apostolic foundation is the stable and enduring point of reference for the church, on which everything depends.

There can be no other gospel, no new gospel (Gal 1:7). We are bound to the faith that has been transmitted once and for all (Jude 3), the apostolic doctrine and inheritance (*parathēkē, depositum*: I Tim 6:20; 2 Tim 1:12, 14), and we ourselves must hand this on faithfully. This is why "preserving" (Luke 11:28; John 12:47; Acts 16:4; I Tim 5:21) and "remaining" (John 8:31; I John 2:6, 27, etc.) are basic verbs in the New Testament, and a one-sided progressive attitude is excluded a priori. The last book in the New Testament formulates a principle that is already attested in the Old Testament: one may neither add anything nor take anything away (Deut 4:2; 13:1; Rev 22:18f.; *Didache* 4.13).

This fidelity to the apostolic origin has often been dismissed as backwoods conservatism, as obstinacy, as a lack of flexibility, or as hostility to progress. We may confidently reply that it is precisely this fidelity that ensures that we will not be abandoned to every wind of quickly changing fashions and opinions (Eph 4:14). One whose only desire is to keep up with the latest fashion will soon himself be unfashionable; but the apostolic foundation offers us a stable and sure standpoint. Others may regard the gospel that has been transmitted once and for all as folly, but for us it is the power and wisdom of God—and the alleged folly of God is wiser than human wisdom (1 Cor 1:23f.). It is our task not merely to hand on this gift like a lifeless coin but to demonstrate that it is indeed the power and wisdom of God, which shows us the way ahead and helps us to master the future.

The Church's Faith:
An Inheritance Received from the Apostles

As the introduction to Luke's Gospel shows, the church's fidelity to her origin led her at an early date to collect the words of the Lord (Luke 1:1-4); similarly, the Letters of Paul were sent from one community to another to be read aloud (Col 4:16), and the Second Letter of Peter knows a collection of "all the letters of our beloved brother Paul" (3:15f.). The final definition of the biblical canon was an act of reception in which the church consciously took her stance under the apostolic origin and made this the criterion (*kanōn* in Greek).

This is why the church has always venerated scripture as sacred, just as she has always venerated the Body of the

Lord as sacred (*Dei Verbum* 21). Scripture is the mirror in which the church must continually scrutinize herself (*Dei Verbum* 7); the Second Vatican Council expressed the desire that scripture form the criterion for everything in the church's preaching and praxis, since scripture is the soul of theology (*Dei Verbum* 21-25). This means that the reading and pondering of scripture must have a central role in the life of every priest: the source and inspiration of his preaching and his entire work must be the Word of God, not private ideas of his own (*Presbyterorum Ordinis* 4; 13). The council quotes Saint Jerome, the learned exegete and church father: "Ignorance of the scriptures means ignorance of Christ" (*Dei Verbum* 25).

Since the Word of God is alive, creative, and life-giving, Christianity is not a "religion of a book," and faithfulness to the Word of God, which is attested in scripture, has nothing in common with a narrow-minded fundamentalism. This is because the apostles not only bequeathed individual sayings that were then passed on from mouth to mouth; nor did they only leave us individual writings, although these are undoubtedly important, valuable, and sacred to us. Rather, their words took shape in a living faith and in the praxis of this faith, especially in the liturgy of the church, which was called into life by their preaching and by the testimony of their lives. In the church and through the church, Jesus Christ continues to work in the Holy Spirit; in her and through her, we hear his word today.

Accordingly, Paul writes to the Corinthians: "You yourselves are our letter, written on our hearts, to be known and read by all; and you show that you are a letter of Christ, prepared by us, written not with ink but with the Spirit of the living God, not on tablets of stone but on tablets of human hearts" (2 Cor 3:2f.). These words have left a deep and enduring imprint on the church's tradition.

One of the first witnesses to this tradition, Irenaeus of Lyons, wrote toward the end of the second century that many barbarian peoples had written the tradition on their hearts, without paper and ink (*Adversus haereses* 3.4.2), and we find the same tradition in great theologians such as Origen and Thomas Aquinas. For Thomas, the law of the gospel (*lex evangelii*) is a written law (*lex scripta*) only in a secondary phase; it is primarily an infused law (*lex indita*), "the grace of the Holy Spirit which is bestowed through faith in Christ" (*Summa theologiae* I/II 106.1). Cardinal Marcello Cervini, one of the presidents at the Council of Trent, which discussed the positions taken by the Reformation theologians, wrote that the apostolic faith is not transmitted to us *in carta* ("on paper"), but is inscribed by the Holy Spirit *in cordibus fidelium,* "on the hearts of the faithful." Accordingly, the council concluded that "the Gospel in the church" is the "source of all saving truth and ethical order" (Denziger-Schönmetzer, *Enchiridion Symbolorum,* 1501).

In the nineteenth century, the Tübingen School (especially Johann Sebastian Drey and Johann Adam Moehler) renewed this profound understanding of tradition and of the church. They understood tradition as the act whereby Jesus Christ transmits himself to us and becomes an abiding presence. This line of thought led to the affirmations of the Second Vatican Council (*Dei Verbum* 7-10) and remains fruitful today. From my student days onward, I have been an adherent of this Tübingen tradition. As J. R. Geiselmann, one of my professors, said, its great concern is a living faith nourished by the sanctified tradition.

This position sees the church of the living God as the pillar and bulwark of the truth (1 Tim 3:15). It was the church that preserved, collected, and handed on the apostolic writings, and this means that one cannot interpret them on one's own initiative: they must be expounded in that apostolic spirit which lives on in the church in so many ways. It is, of course, true that the church must remain in the truth which has been handed on once and for all, and must examine herself continually in the light of the scriptures, which are inspired by the Spirit of God. The Second Letter of Peter already warns against a do-it-yourself interpretation (2 Pet 1:20f.). The earliest Christians saw unanimity as a proof of authenticity (Acts 1:14; 2:46; 4:24, etc.), and this remains an important criterion for the correct interpretation of the apostolic testimony.

Taking the apostolic origin as our point of reference is thus a many-layered process of interpretation, in which many voices must be heard—those before our own days, and those contemporary with us—under the guidance of the apostolic ministry. The binding interpretation of the apostolic faith is possible only when all these voices resound in harmony, for as Hans Urs von Balthasar memorably said, the truth is symphonic.

The schisms in the course of church history had their origin in unauthorized expositions of scripture, whereas the renewal movements were born when scripture was read in the church and in her spirit. For example, Francis of Assisi asked Pope Innocent III for permission to live with his brothers as the apostles had lived. And the only viable path to renewal today is reflection on the apostolic origin, in order to find a path ahead in fellowship with the entire church, which is built on the foundation of the apostles.

Apostolic Succession as Apostolic Mission

Of its very nature, the apostolic ministry is unique. This is why—despite what some sects assume—there can be no new apostles after the first ones. However, the missionary command with which Matthew's Gospel closes tells us that the apostles are sent out to the farthest reaches of the earth and the end of time (Matt 28:19f.; cf. Acts 1:8). This obliged the apostles during their lifetime to appoint men who could take up their apostolic mission and continue it after the apostles themselves were dead. The apostolic succession is thus rooted in the eschatological and universal character of the work and mission of Jesus Christ.

These successors of the apostles are not new apostles. They are obligated to the faith that was transmitted once and for all (Jude 3) and to the inheritance that comes from the apostles, and they in turn must hand this on faithfully. Although they do not have the ministry of apostles, they do have a genuinely apostolic ministry, because they carry out some of the apostles' tasks, especially that of witnessing to the apostolic inheritance that has been handed on once and for all. Naturally, the apostolic patrimony is not congealed into cold stone. Just as the preaching of Jesus and of the apostles was the work of men whose life gave testimony to their words, so too the transmission of this patrimony requires *living* witnesses. The New Testament tells us that these witnesses were publicly appointed; their names are mentioned. Wherever Paul came, he instituted elders by the laying on of hands, accompanied by fasting and prayer (Acts 14:23). In the Pastoral Letters, he exhorts his pupils Timothy and Titus to hand on to others the grace that they have received through the laying on of hands (1 Tim 4:14; 2 Tim 1:6; Titus 1:5; cf. Acts 14:23).

We see that what was later called the "apostolic succession" is essentially present already in the New Testament, and this allowed the theological principle to be formulated explicitly at a very early date, in the postapostolic period. It is attested at the end of the first century, in the letter of Clement of Rome to the community in Corinth (1 Clement 42), and a century later in Tertullian

*The apostolic patrimony is not congealed into cold
stone. Just as the preaching of Jesus and of the
apostles was the work of men whose life gave
testimony to their words, so too the transmission
of this patrimony requires living witnesses.*

(*De praescriptione* 21); but the chief witness is Irenaeus of
Lyons, who develops a theology of the apostolic succession:

"The tradition of the apostles, which is visible
throughout the world, can be seen in every church by anyone who wants to see the truth, and we can list the bishops who were appointed by the bishops in the individual
churches, and their successors down to our own days"
(*Adversus haereses* 3.3.1). Irenaeus sees the apostolic succession as the guarantee that the individual churches remain
in the tradition of the apostolic faith: "Through this
ordering and this succession, the tradition which has been
present in the church from the time of the apostles and
the preaching of the truth have come down to us"
(3.3.3). In this process, a particular importance attaches
to the testimony of the church of Rome, which was
founded by Peter and Paul, and whose successors are well
known (3.3.2).

Irenaeus does not see the apostolic succession as a kind
of pipeline; his thinking is pneumatological. According
to the Gospel of John, it is the Spirit himself who
reminds the disciples of all that Jesus said and did; by
means of this remembrance, he leads the disciples into
the fullness of truth (John 14:26; 15:26; 16:13). There is
thus a close link between the recollection that looks back
to the origin and the forward-looking initiation into
deeper dimensions. Irenaeus takes up this pneumatological perspective and writes that it is the Holy Spirit who

always preserves the youthful freshness of the faith in the church (*Adversus haereses* 3.24.1).

The Spirit ensures that the truth of the gospel never becomes old or obsolete. In its inexhaustible richness, it is always young, and continually rejuvenates, stimulates, and inspires the church. We need a new spiritual exodus today, firmly anchored in the original testimony of the apostles, united to the fellowship of the church, and filled with the Holy Spirit, who—according to the promise made to the prophet Ezekiel (chap. 37)—awakens the dry dead bones to life and breathes a new spirit into them.

When he opened the Second Vatican Council, Pope John XXIII predicted such a renewed and renewing Pentecost, and we are now seeing the first signs of this, as Pope John Paul II and Pope Benedict XVI affirmed when they met the members of the spiritual movements at the Pentecost Vigils in 1998 and 2006. At the same time, however, we also see symptoms of paralysis in today's church, a lack of courage and of joy in the faith. These deficiencies smother all missionary vigor and prevent the emergence of any vision that is open to the future.

Faithfulness to the origin means that we priests must be faithful to our mission to the whole world. This is not only a geographical reality; we encounter everywhere "worlds" in which the gospel has not yet taken root, or where these roots have dried up. Here I have in mind the spheres of science and culture, of economics and politics, of the media and the world of sport. If we ask what form the new evangelization can take, there is no easy answer; still less can we propose one answer that would be valid everywhere. At any rate, however, one thing is clear: the apostolic succession does not mean a comfortable life. It is a commission that imposes an obligation on us. As an apostolic church, the church is essentially missionary (*Ad Gentes* 2).

Fellow Workers of the Apostles

How are we to bring about such an exodus? Do we have the personnel required? One first answer lies in the permanently valid words of Jesus: "The harvest is plentiful, but the laborers are few; therefore ask the Lord of the harvest to send out laborers into his harvest" (Matt 9:37; Luke 10:2). We cannot simply "produce" these workers or organize their supply: we must pray for them and receive them as a gift. The New Testament gives a second pointer when it tells us that the first bearers of the apostolic responsibility were never isolated. They were no soloists waging a solitary fight; they were surrounded and supported by a group of committed and responsible fellow workers. In today's circumstances, we too need such a group of people.

In the New Testament period, the apostles' fellow workers included outstanding men, such as Stephen (Acts 6:5, 8-15; 7) and Philip (Acts 6:5; 8:4-40; 21:8), who were full of the Holy Spirit. We meet Paul's traveling companions, especially Barnabas, Silas, Mark, Timothy, Titus, and Luke. We also hear of prophets, teachers, and evangelists (Acts 13:1; 21:8; I Cor 12:28; Eph 4:11f.; 2 Tim 4:5). Nor should we forget the deacons (Phil 1:1; I Tim 3:8-13). There is an impressively long list of the men and women who were Paul's fellow workers (Romans 16; I Cor 16:15-20; Col 4:7-17; 2 Tim 4:19-21; Philemon 1f., 23); these include the married couple Aquila and Prisca, who are often mentioned. They were a great help to the apostle in various places (Acts 18:2; Rom 16:3; I Cor 16:19; 2 Tim 4:19).

It is noteworthy how many women are mentioned in Acts (16:14, 40; 18:2, 18) and in the Letters of Paul (above all in Romans 16). Their active and important collaboration is explicitly acknowledged, and this is in keeping with the behavior of Jesus himself, who was accompanied by women who used their private means to support him and his disciples (Luke 8:2f.; 23:49). Some of them were the first witnesses to the resurrection (Matt 28:5-10; Mark 16:9; Luke 24:10, 22; John 20:11-18). The most important of these women was Mary of Magdala, and this is why tradition calls her the first Easter witness and *apostola apostolorum*, "the female apostle of the male apostles."

The Catholic Church bases her belief that she is not entitled to ordain women to the priesthood on the fact that the New Testament shows us women carrying out important tasks but not women called to be members of the twelve or of the group of apostles. Many people (and not only women) find this argument hard or impossible to follow. If, however, one takes seriously the fact that the New Testament shows us women carrying out many other responsible tasks, one cannot say that the church's position is hostile to women. Rather, it corresponds to the fact that men and women are different but possess the same dignity and are equal in rank.

It is not correct to say that this biblical testimony to the responsible collaboration of women was forgotten, or even intentionally suppressed, in later church history. There can be no doubt that cultural factors led to a lower esteem for women, but the church repeatedly broke through those cultural barriers, and history shows many examples of women whose prophetical and mystical gifts and whose charitable initiatives made an immense contribution to the church's apostolic work. Without them, the church would have taken a completely different course.

Alongside Benedict we find his sister, Scholastica; alongside Boniface, his companions Lioba and Walburga; alongside Francis we have Clare; alongside Francis de Sales we have Jane Frances de Chantal; alongside Vincent de Paul we find Louise de Marillac; and Don Bosco's mother was just as important in his life as was Monica in the life of Saint Augustine. We can draw up a lengthy list of women who have influenced church history: from Hildegard of Bingen, Catherine of Siena, Bridget of Sweden, and Elizabeth of Hungary in the Middle Ages down to Mother Teresa of Calcutta in our own days. We recall women mystics who have had a lasting impact on the spirituality of the church, such as Juliana of Liège, Teresa of Avila, Margaret Mary Alacoque, or Thérèse of Lisieux. There can be no doubt that in our new missionary situation women have important tasks, and this is why it is vital to support their responsible collaboration in the church.

In addition to the fellow workers of the apostles, the New Testament also knows community apostles, that is, emissaries who were commissioned as delegates of the local churches (2 Cor 8:23; Phil 2:25). According to one textual variant, these included a female apostle named Junia (Rom 16:7), who was clearly either a delegate of one community or else an itinerant preacher of the gospel.

We hear once again of itinerant apostles in the period immediately subsequent to the New Testament (*Didache* 11.3-6), and they reappear in a new form in the nomadic Irish and Scottish monks of the sixth century to whom so many places in western Europe owe their Christian faith. In this sense, some bishops, priests, and laymen and women are called apostles. Boniface is known as the apostle of the Germans, and Cyril and Methodius as the apostles of the Slavs. Men and women inspired by apostolic zeal and commitment are often called apostles among the workers, or the poor or the sick; and young people can be apostles among the youth.

It is important for bishops and priests to promote this apostolic zeal and to support the apostolic initiatives and work of others. In the new missionary situation, it is urgent to awaken and to discover missionary charisms. We must go in search of the lost, the alienated, those who have wandered away from the fold (Luke 15). Like Paul, we too must be present in the Areopagus of contemporary culture and the marketplaces of our world today (see Acts 17:22).

In order to tackle these new challenges, we must find responsible fellow workers, train them, support them; and, above all, we must trust them. Anyone who has even a little apostolic experience knows that the collaboration with committed fellow workers is one of the most agreeable aspects of pastoral work. Such men and women are a true gift of God, for which we can never be sufficiently thankful. They deserve a greater measure of public recognition than we usually give them!

4

The Priest as a Man of the Spirit

The Development of the Threefold Ministry

After the council, and especially in the aftermath of the upheavals associated with the year 1968, there was a lively and sometimes stormy discussion of the postapostolic ecclesial ministries: their historical genesis, the correct way to understand them, their practical exercise, the appropriate lifestyle for the ordained ministries, and their hierarchical structure. Similar discussions took place in the medieval debates and demands for church reform, and the controversies with Reformation theology, and they continue in a new way in our modern ecumenical conversations. Things may have calmed down somewhat in the Catholic Church, but this does not mean that these questions have been settled once and for all. My remarks in this chapter are meant only as suggestions for further reflection. We shall follow the tracks in history and look for the path that can take us into the future.

The biblical and historical questions are very complex, but it is indisputable that we find a variety of ministries in the New Testament communities. Very early on, when their tasks threatened to overburden the apostles, they appointed the "seven" by the laying on of hands to help them and to guide the Gentile Christian communities (Acts 6:1-7). Wherever Paul came, he appointed "elders" (*presbyteroi*) by the laying on of hands, accompanied by fasting and prayer (Acts 14:23). In view of his approaching death, he bade farewell to Ephesus and appointed pastors who had been instituted by the Holy Spirit; these are called both *episkopoi* and *presbyteroi.* After his departure, they were to watch over the flock (Acts 20:28f.). He gives the same charge to Timothy and Titus in his Pastoral Letters (I Tim 4:14; 2 Tim 1:6; Titus 1:5).

In the Jewish Christian groups, the men who headed the communities are called *presbyteroi* on the model of the synagogue, where elders were appointed in the communities (Acts 14:23; 15:2; 20:17, etc.; James 5:14; I Tim 5:17; Titus 1:5). The English word *priest* (like the German *Priester,* the French *prêtre,* and the Italian *prete*) is derived from the Greek *presbyteros.* In the Gentile Christian groups, we hear of *episkopoi,* literally "overseers," that is, men who have the task of supervision and keeping everything under control (Acts 20:28; Phil 1:1; I Tim 3:2). The English word *bishop* (like the German *Bischof,* the French *évêque,* and the Italian *vescovo*) is derived from the Greek *episkopos;* the title "superintendent," which is still common in European Protestant usage, comes from the Latin *superintendens* and expresses the same task. The concept of "shepherd/pastor" is used in the New Testament to give a more precise definition of the concepts of *presbyteroi* and *episkopoi* (Acts 20:28; I Pet 2:25; 5:2); the title "pastor" and the concept of "pastoral work" derive from this.

This shows that there was never any initial period in the church without official ministries: these have existed from the outset. Nevertheless, the texts to which I have referred here show that they did not have a uniform structure at the beginning. It is, of course, anachronistic to draw a parallel between this situation and the church orders of the different confessions today, or to appeal to the New Testament to legitimate our present-day situation. The fact that the two terms *episkopos* and *presbyteros* are juxtaposed in one and the same passage (compare Acts 20:17 with 20:28) shows that what we find in the New Testament are not mutually contradictory church orders, but a legitimate pluralism within a broader consensus.

We see a clear tendency toward uniformity as early as the late writings in the New Testament, which always speak of the "bishop" in the singular and of "presbyters" in the plural. On this basis, the threefold ministry of bishop, priest, and deacon developed in the immediately postapostolic period, which is virtually contemporary with the last writings in the New Testament.

The martyr bishop Ignatius of Antioch, at the beginning of the second century, sees the episcopal constitution as an essential element of the church's structure: "Endeavor to do everything in harmony with God. The bishop, in the place of God, and the priests, in the place of the council of the apostles, are in charge, and the deacons whom I love so dearly are entrusted with the service of Jesus Christ, who was with the Father before time began and was manifested at the end of time" (*Magnesians* 6.1). He writes to the Ephesians: "Thus is it is right to glorify Jesus Christ in every way, since he glorifies you, so that you may be sanctified in all things, bound firmly together in unanimous submission, obedient to the bishop and to the presbyters" (2.2; see 20.2). The college of presbyters should be united to the bishop like the strings of a lyre and form one single harmonious choir (4.1f.).

Ignatius presents an ideal picture that probably does not portray the reality everywhere at that time; but the threefold ministry became the norm in the East and in the West, and met with little resistance. The Second Vatican Council fully confirmed this position (*Lumen Gentium* 29; *Presbyterorum Ordinis* 7). The speed with which the conception of the threefold ministry became the norm and was taken for granted has often prompted the surprising question: What made it so convincing that it was accepted so quickly everywhere? The question whether this threefold ministry is essential often arises in conversation with Christians from the Reformation traditions.

The Spiritual Character of the Priestly Ministry

A purely sociological explanation is obviously incapable of telling us why the threefold ministry developed so quickly. It is not enough to say that certain ministries in the community were necessary from a purely human and sociological perspective in order to ensure that things functioned properly, and that this is why the Jewish Christians had recourse to the community structure of the synagogue with its *presbyteroi* and the Gentile Christians had recourse to the *episkopoi*. We are also told that the concepts of *presbyteroi* and *episkopoi* are to be understood functionally, and that this shows that the early Christian ministries were not understood in priestly terms, but only in functional terms. The argument then is that since we today live in a different world, we can and indeed must have recourse to other "leadership philosophies."

This explanation seems obvious, but only at first sight. As soon as we begin to examine it, we realize that it does not do justice to the New Testament data. As we have seen, one receives a ministry in the New Testament in a liturgical form, by means of the laying on of hands and prayer. It is the Holy Spirit himself who appoints the bishops (Acts 20:28), and this means that the laying on of hands is not to be understood as an external gesture, a rite with a purely legal significance. It bestows a special

charism, the Spirit of power, of love, and of self-control
(2 Tim 1:6f.; cf. I Tim 4:14). Ultimately, it is the exalted
Lord himself who appoints pastors in the church (Eph
4:11) and works through them. This is why the apostle
can go so far as to speak of "God's fellow workers" (*syn-
ergoi*) (I Cor 3:9; I Thess 3:2; see 2 Cor 1:24).

As early as the New Testament, therefore, we find all
the essential elements of a sacramental understanding of
the ecclesial ministry. Just as God was present and worked
among us in a visible human form in Jesus Christ, so too
the exalted Lord works in the Holy Spirit in and through
visible signs. "That which was visible in Jesus Christ has
passed into the sacraments" (Pope Leo the Great, *Sermon*
74.2).

The sacramental foundation of the ministries does not
contradict a charismatic church order. It is, in fact, an
essential constitutive element of such an ordering, when
this is rightly understood. The First Letter to the
Corinthians has often been expounded as presenting a
purely charismatic church order, but this text itself calls
the ministry of leadership a charism (I Cor 12:28), and
the community is urged to acknowledge and submit to
those whose function is leadership (16:16-18; cf. Heb
13:7, 17).

Paul compares the many various charisms, services, and
ministries in the church to an organism in which each
member has its own specific function, but can carry this
out only in collaboration with all the others (I Cor 12:4-

27). Accordingly, there should be an orderly interplay of the various charisms, services, and ministries in the church. Here, the priest has his own irreplaceable function, which he cannot delegate to anyone else, and which the others must respect. The others too, however, have their charism and task, which the priest in turn must respect. Since this interplay involves sinful persons, it may occasionally by spoiled in the church by fouls and other breaches of the rules; but it has its own order, structure, and logic, which constitute its inner and outer beauty. The church is a structured body in the Holy Spirit. She is a body (I Cor 12:12-31; Eph 4:15f.; Col 2:19) and a building in the Holy Spirit (Eph 2:21f.; I Pet 2:5; cf. I Cor 3:9).

This means that the empirical external structure that the sociologist can study has christological and pneumatological foundations. This entitles the church to understand the development of the structure of her ministries as the work of the Holy Spirit. This is not a purely human organization: to use the language of a later theological period, it belongs not to the sphere of human law but to that of divine law. Accordingly, the ministers in the church speak and act not in their own names but in the name of Jesus Christ himself (Matt 10:40; Luke 10:16), and what Paul says of himself applies to them too: "We are ambassadors for Christ, since God is making his appeal through us; we entreat you on behalf of Christ, be reconciled to God" (2 Cor 5:20).

This lofty claim can, of course, be misunderstood and abused. But the christological and pneumatological foundation of the ministry is important not only in view of its unique position in the church but also for everything concerned with the exercise of the ministry. The priest's ministry ought to be permeated by its christological origin: it should be in conformity to the basic attitude of Jesus, who came not to rule but to serve, and who laid down this principle for his disciples too (Mark 10:42-45). Office-bearers in the church ought not to exercise their ministerial charism arrogantly and highhandedly. Like all the charisms, theirs must be understood as helping to build up the community (I Cor 12:7; Eph 4:12). They are not to lord it over other people's faith, but are to be servants of their joy (2 Cor 1:24).

When Jesus washed his disciples' feet on the evening before his passion and death, he gave us an example of this servant ministry (John 13:1ff.). "You call me Teacher and Lord—and you are right, for that is what I am. So if I, your Lord and Teacher, have washed your feet, you also ought to wash one another's feet. For I have set you an example, that you also should do as I have done to you" (13:13-15). Priests and bishops must be spiritual men who understand their hierarchical office as a service (*diakonia*).

The First Letter of Peter expresses this idea eloquently: "Tend the flock of God that is in your charge, exercising the oversight, not under compulsion but willingly, as God would have you do it—not for sordid gain, but eagerly. Do not lord it over those in your charge, but be examples to your flock" (5:2f.). This last exhortation is even more impressive in the original Greek: it tells the office-bearers to be the *typoi*, models on whom the communities can pattern their lives. This means that they must not be content to bear witness with their mouths: their whole existence must be a proclamation. The Latin translation expresses this with incomparable skill: *forma facti gregis ex animo* (I Pet 5:3). We might roughly translate this as follows: the form of the priest's life is meant to form and leave its imprint on the community.

The priest cannot carry out this service as an arrogant lord over his parish. He must take the apostles as his model: at the apostolic council in Jerusalem, they involved the entire community in the consultation (Acts 15:22), thereby laying down a pattern to be followed in conciliar discussions. According to the biblical tradition, a wise king will ask for advice and accept good advice. Ignatius of Antioch emphasizes the authority of the bishop more strongly than anyone else in the early church, but he also mentions the assembly (*synedrion*) of the bishop and the priests (*Thrallians* 3.1; *Philadelphians* 8.1). In the same way, the martyr bishop Cyprian writes that he would never do anything without the counsel of the priests and the assent of the people of God (*Letter* 14).

If we wish to know the meaning of spiritual authority and consultation, we will find a valuable answer in the chapters about the abbot and his council in the *Rule* of Saint Benedict, which display a great wisdom and are surely the best words ever written about the exercise of spiritual authority (chaps. 2 and 3). Benedict writes that the abbot should "listen to the advice of the brothers, and then reflect by himself and do what he thinks to be right." He says explicitly that the abbot should listen to *all*, "since the Lord often reveals the better path to one who is younger."

The *Rule* of Saint Benedict can easily be applied by analogy to the bishop in relation to his priests, and to the parish priest in relation to his fellow workers. The Second Vatican Council took an important step in this direction when it revived the synodal structures. There is no doubt that the priest must make decisions in a spiritual manner; the same is even more true of the bishop. But this means that they must first listen to what the Spirit says to the churches (Rev 2:7, 11, 17, 29, etc.). A genuinely spiritual exercise of authority has never been possible without consulting one's confreres and fellow workers. This must not be misunderstood today: what is involved in the authoritative spiritual decision that is taken after consulting and listening to others is not democratization. It is intimately linked to the spiritual character of the ministry and is needed on every level of the church's life.

The priest must make decisions in a spiritual manner; the same is even more true of the bishop. But this means that they must first listen to what the Spirit says to the churches. A genuinely spiritual exercise of authority has never been possible without consulting one's confreres and fellow workers.

Celibacy for the Kingdom of God

The spiritual character of the priest's ministry of service requires a spiritual lifestyle. This has been the subject of many discussions and debates in recent decades, especially with regard to the celibacy of priests and the relevant legislation in canon law. This question is not new; problems arose again and again in the past, and there have been many heated debates. For example, when Pope Gregory VII demanded that priests live in celibacy, Saint Walter of Pontoise defended this at a synod in Paris ca. 1074. Not only was he thrown out; he was soundly thrashed as well.

In today's discussions, the decisive perspective is often lost to view: Jesus himself went against the life expected of a Jewish rabbi, by remaining unmarried. He esteemed marriage highly as a form of life rooted in God's creation, and he gave it a new dignity when he preached about the kingdom of God; later, his teaching led the church to call marriage a sacrament. Consequently, the fact that he himself did not marry and that he called celibacy for the sake of the kingdom of heaven a charism that is "given" and must be freely accepted (Matt 19:11f.) is no devaluation of marriage. On the contrary, when Jesus acknowledges celibacy as an acceptable way of life alongside marriage, he is declaring that in the perspective of God's kingdom, marriage is no longer a necessity imposed by nature and society: it is a way of life that can be chosen freely.

Celibacy does not devalue marriage: it gives it a *higher* value.

It is correct to say that most likely all the apostles other than Paul were married. Paul himself explicitly defends the right of the other apostles to be accompanied by a believing wife (1 Cor 9:5). The New Testament also assumes that the *episkopoi* and *presbyteroi* are married and have families (1 Tim 3:2, 4; Titus 1:6). This means that priestly celibacy is neither a divine commandment nor an apostolic ordinance. It does, however, correspond to a spiritual experience in the church that goes back more than fifteen hundred years. And even the postapostolic church accepted the apostle's advice (1 Cor 7:25) and recognized that celibacy, as an undivided service for the sake of the kingdom of heaven and "for the things of the Lord" (1 Cor 7:33f.), is highly appropriate for priests. This form of the imitation of Jesus gives an inner and outer freedom for the undivided service of the gospel, because one is spared many worldly cares and need not consider the needs of one's family (1 Cor 7:28-35). It is one way to "leave all things" (Mark 10:28f.) in order to spend all one's life in fellowship and friendship with Jesus and to be sent out everywhere by him.

This is why it is wrong to assert (as we so often hear) that the tradition of celibacy in the Latin church emerged only at the beginning of the second millennium. Exhortations and regulations in this sense, initially dealing with abstinence from sexual relations within marriage and then

directly with celibacy, go back to a much earlier period.
The canons of the synod of Elvira in Spain (ca. 306/
309), like other synods of that time, speak of the clerics'
obligation to practice abstinence. They presuppose an
older tradition; they are not introducing new laws, but
only insisting that existing laws be observed. This brings
us with historical certainty back into the immediately
postapostolic age. The Second Vatican Council set its seal
on this tradition, which is now more than fifteen centuries old, and explicitly confirmed the law of celibacy
(*Presbyterorum Ordinis* 16).

Today, it is difficult for many people to grasp that
celibacy, when freely chosen for the sake of the kingdom
of heaven, is an eschatological sign, and there are many
reasons for this. To begin with, we live in a world in which
sex and the erotic are omnipresent to an extent never seen
before, and the celibate life consequently demands a high
degree of human maturity. More pedagogical and psychological preparation is needed today than in the past,
and the priest needs more help. One can only wish that
every priest will meet women with whom he can form
friendships—women who have the maturity and magna-
nimity required in order to respect and support the spiritual lifestyle of the priest.

An equally difficult problem is posed by the fact that
a world closed in upon itself finds a lifestyle that seeks to
be an eschatological sign alien and incomprehensible,
indeed offensive, and suspicion is cast openly on those

who choose to live in such a way. It would, however, be quite wrong to accept this mentality uncritically: precisely in such a situation, celibacy can be very *modern* as a sign and a challenge. The freedom to let oneself be sent anywhere, without needing to take one's own family into account, is in accordance with a church that is preparing herself for a new missionary exodus.

Naturally, one who proposes to lead such a life in today's world must really know who he is, in human and in spiritual terms. No one can achieve this consolidation of his identity on his own: we need the fellowship of our confreres and spiritual direction, especially in times of crisis. Many priests today live as singles, but this leads to an inhuman and un-Christian loneliness that does not in the least correspond to the lifestyle of Jesus, who lived in fellowship with others. This makes the question of new forms of the *vita communis* particularly urgent; I shall return to this below.

Not only celibacy is in crisis: the same is true of marriage, understood and lived in the Christian spirit. In the past, vocations to celibacy came from good Christian families, just as good priests were always a great help to married couples and families. This too shows how marriage and celibacy support each other—and how both are affected by today's crisis. We live in a society where the Christian values that once provided support in the realm of sexuality, marriage, and family are crumbling, and we are forced to ask how these two lifestyles can survive. The problem of a Christian lifestyle today concerns priests and laypeople equally. It must be addressed by *both* together, if we are to find a solution.

A Spiritual Lifestyle

Most discussions of celibacy make the mistake of viewing the problem in isolation. But voluntary celibacy can be understood and lived only within the total context of a spiritual lifestyle—that is, a life in which the Spirit guides us (Rom 8:4f.; Gal 5:16, 25), a life "in keeping with the Spirit," not in keeping with the criteria of "this world," an orientation that follows "the Spirit of Christ" (Rom 8:9). In the last analysis, it is Jesus Christ himself who lives in us and works through us (Gal 2:20).

The most important element in a spiritual lifestyle is an atmosphere of prayer. Jesus himself always withdrew for prayer in the decisive moments of his earthly life. He often prayed alone on a mountain (Matt 14:43) or in a lonely place (Luke 9:18), even when everyone was looking for him (Mark 1:37). He taught his disciples how to pray. Indeed, he initiated them into a school of prayer (Matt 6:9-13; Luke 11:1-13). He exhorted them to pray unceasingly (Luke 18:1), but without using a multitude of words (Matt 6:7). After his ascension, the disciples gathered and prayed with one voice (Acts 1:13f.); later on, the first Christians assembled regularly for prayer (Acts 2:46). In critical situations, for example, when

James was executed and Peter was put in prison, they prayed with special intensity (Acts 12:5).

Paul sees prayer as an essential part of his apostolic ministry. He repeatedly mentions his prayer for his communities (1 Thess 1:2; 3:10; 2 Thess 1:3, etc.), and he often asks them to pray for him (Rom 15:30; Col 4:3; 1 Thess 5:25; 2 Thess 3:1). Similarly, a priest will pray for and with his community, and it is absolutely vital for him to be borne up by their prayer for him. If he does not pray, he cannot teach others how to pray—and this seems to me a primary task of the priest. Many people today want to pray, but they cannot do so because they do not know how.

In addition to prayer, a spiritual lifestyle must be molded by the spirit of the Beatitudes in the Sermon on the Mount (Matt 5:2-11; Luke 6:20-26), which are basic for every state of life in the church, including the priesthood. We must also recall the instructions Jesus gives to his disciples when he sends them out, especially the requirement that they lead a simple life in material terms (Mark 6:6-13 par.; Luke 10:1-12), and Jesus' criticism of those who seek titles (Matt 23:8) and rank (Mark 10:33-37 par.)—we would say, of those who want an ecclesiastical career. Jesus castigates greed (Mark 10:17-31 par.), the desire to dominate others, and the yearning for power and influence (Mark 10:35-45 par.). Celibacy for the kingdom of heaven means a life in poverty, making few material demands, for the sake of the kingdom, and *this* raises at least as many urgent questions about the priestly lifestyle as the issue of celibacy itself.

Finally, a spiritual lifestyle involves forms of fellowship among brothers and sisters. Jesus called his disciples personally, but not as isolated individuals. His lifestyle was that of a community, and this must be true of the priestly existence too. Through priestly ordination, we are all given a share in the one *ordo* and become members of the one *presbyterium.* We call one another "confreres." This is why priests should meet and should visit one another, sharing their pastoral experiences (whether good or bad), consoling and strengthening one another in priestly solidarity. There should be genuine friendships among priests. It is a great pity that modern bourgeois individualism has made such inroads among priests today! Communities of priests such as the "Jesus Caritas" fellowship of Charles de Foucauld, the Schönstatt priests, or the Focolare priests can help enrich our spiritual lives.

We are still searching for the form that the priestly lifestyle will take in the future. Sociological changes have not stopped short at the door to priests' houses; the rectories of yesterday have almost all ceased to exist, and we do not yet know what will take their place. But many young families face similar problems. Both clergy and laity are searching for the specific form of Christian and ecclesial spiritual life in accordance with the gospel, and this is a challenge that we must tackle together. I shall return to this question in a wider context toward the end of this book.

– 5 –

Priestly Ministry as Pastoral Ministry

Jesus Christ—The Good Shepherd

In the tumultuous years after the council, I attempted to interpret the ministry of priestly service as leadership of the community on the model of the biblical understanding of the ministry of "shepherd" (*pastor* in Latin). When I wrote about leadership, therefore, I was referring to the pastoral dimension of the priestly ministry, which obviously is the heart of very many priests' activity. But what does "pastoral" mean? Various and sometimes contradictory answers are given to this question. Some see "pastoral" as almost a magical word that will solve all our problems, while others see it as a blurring of theological realities, because a pastoral care oriented to human beings is often understood one-sidedly as a response to human needs instead of pastoral care oriented to the Word of God and to the truth. Let us therefore look more closely at the biblical image of shepherd in order to clarify the genuine and profound meaning of pastoral ministry.

When the Bible speaks of shepherds, this has nothing to do with the pastoral idylls of Romanticism. From the time of the patriarchs onward, shepherds were regarded in Israel as great leaders and guides whose task was to show the way. They protected not only a herd but the whole clan against dangers of every kind, and led them to good pastures. They looked after both human beings and animals, and took account of their condition. They were both masters and companions.

In the Old Testament, Yahweh is called the shepherd of his people. The Psalms speak movingly of God's guidance and loving care: "The Lord is my shepherd, I shall not want. He makes me lie down in green pastures; he leads me beside still waters. . . . Even though I walk through the darkest valley, I fear no evil" (Ps 23:1-2, 4). "For he is our God, and we are the people of his pasture, and the sheep of his hand" (95:7; cf. 78:52-54; 80:2). The prophet says of Yahweh: "He will feed his flock like a shepherd; he will gather the lambs in his arms, and carry them in his bosom, and gently lead the mother sheep" (Isa 40:11).

As a caring shepherd, God entrusts his sheep to his servants, to Moses (Ps 77:2), David (Ps 78:70-72), and others. The shepherds appointed by God, however, did not look after the flock, but pastured only their own selves, letting the flock be scattered (Ezek 34:1-10). "The wind shall shepherd all your shepherds" (Jer 22:22). This is why Yahweh will once again take the flock into his own hands (Ezek 34:11-22) and give them shepherds after his own heart (Jer 3:15; 23:4).

In the spirit of these words, Jesus is aware of having been sent as shepherd to the lost sheep of Israel (Luke 15:24; cf. 10:6). He is filled with compassion when he sees the people, who are like sheep without a shepherd (Mark 6:34). He understands himself as the shepherd who goes in search of the lost sheep. When he finds it, he takes it on his shoulders and brings it home full of joy. And he knows that this causes great joy in heaven (Luke 15:4-10).

The Gospel of John elaborates a shepherd christology all of its own (John 10). Jesus calls himself the good (i.e., the true) shepherd who knows his own, just as they know him. Unlike the hired hands, he does not abandon his flock when thieves and robbers come; he lays down his life for his sheep. He leads them and keeps them together, and brings them to good pastures where they find life in abundance (10:10).

Other New Testament writings likewise take up the motif of shepherd and call Jesus Christ "the great shepherd of the sheep" (Heb 13:20), the "arch-shepherd" (1 Pet 5:4), or "the shepherd and bishop of our souls" (1 Pet 2:25). This motif is found throughout the New

Testament, and early Christian iconography, above all the depictions of Christ in the catacombs, shows that it had an inherent credibility that evoked a response in believers from the very beginning.

"I Will Send You Shepherds"

Jesus is not only the "arch-shepherd"; he also sends shepherds. According to the New Testament, he is the exalted Lord who appoints them from heaven (Eph 4:11). They are identical with the *presbyteroi* and *episkopoi* (Acts 20:28; 1 Pet 2:25; 5:2), and so their ministry is understood as "pastoral." The New Testament views this as a serious matter, for at the end they must give an account to Christ the pastor and "arch-shepherd" (1 Pet 5:4). Indeed, community leaders will be called more rigorously to account at the judgment (Heb 13:17).

First of all, the shepherd must know the path and show it to others, giving them a goal and an orientation. He must confront them with the choice between the two paths: the steep path that leads to salvation and the broad highway that leads to damnation (Matt 7:13f.; Luke 13:24; see *Didache* 1-6). He must know—and also say!— that only Jesus Christ is the way, the truth, and the life (John 14:6) and that love is the "excellent way" of Christians (1 Cor 12:31). Only the truth can make us really free (John 8:32); only the truth is the light of life (cf.

John 3:21). In the New Testament, Christianity is defined as the new, that is, the true and definitive, "way" (Acts 9:2; 19:9, 23, etc.). A pastoral service that failed to point out the path would be like a blind person leading other blind persons. They would all fall into a ditch, deserving Nietzsche's mockery: "Who still wants to rule? Who still wants to obey? Both are too much trouble. No shepherd and no flock!"

Since he is the truth, Jesus is also the way. He is the good shepherd who is with us on the way. Accordingly, just as life in general can be called a journey, the Christian existence is a journey and the church is a pilgrim church *en route.* The shepherds must not be hard-hearted: they must go in search of those who wander astray and get lost, those left lying by the wayside, and those who stand afar off. They must care for these persons and bring them home, in the knowledge that this causes joy in heaven (Luke 15:3-7). They must be on their guard against intruders who spread false teachings, and they must look after the weak (Acts 20:30f., 35). They must rejoice with those who rejoice, and weep with those who weep (Rom 12:15). Like the apostle, they must become all things to all people (1 Cor 9:22). In short, their duty is to utter the truth clearly, but they must enact the truth in love (Eph 4:15).

If we take Jesus as our model, pastoral ministry means going in search of others, not waiting passively for them to turn up. When I was a curate, we visited the sick regularly in their homes. We called on families when a death had taken place, and we visited everyone who was new in the parish. Today, this is often no longer possible for a priest, but laypersons can take over this service of visiting. Bishops from countries where the Pentecostal churches and sects are growing by leaps and bounds sometimes tell me, "They are always there when people need help, and they snatch our people away from us." I invariably reply: "But why are we Catholics not there?" Personal contact is essential in pastoral care, and nothing can replace it, not even the friendliest parish newsletters.

The good shepherd will go in search of those who suffer in body and in spirit. His heart will go out to the materially poor and to the poor in spirit, to those who need his words of consolation and advice. He will not always have a concrete solution ready to hand in every situation of distress; he will have to spend a great deal of time simply listening to other people, but this too can be very helpful. Paul describes his ministry as a fatherly service of love and affection (I Cor 4:15; Phil 2:22; Philemon 10). When I was in seminary, we were often told that you can only be a celibate priest if you could equally well have been a good father, a man capable of displaying fatherly concern for children and for those whom the gospel calls the "little ones." It is not by chance that priests are addressed as "Father" in many languages. This word shows both respect and affection.

In addition to his care for the lost, the poor, the weak, and the persecuted, a basic duty of the shepherd is to

Bishops from countries where the Pentecostal churches and sects are growing by leaps and bounds sometimes tell me, "They are always there when people need help, and they snatch our people away from us." I invariably reply: "But why are we Catholics not there?"

gather his flock and keep it together. The priestly ministry serves to promote unity. This is an organizational task only on a secondary level; the decisive thing is the spiritual task. The priest is to gather everyone around the one shepherd, Jesus Christ, and to keep the flock together in the one faith, the one love, and the one hope. He must pay heed to the variety of charisms that are present in the community, ensuring that each charism receives its proper place, so that it can make its distinctive contribution. It would be fatal if some few persons were to exercise a monopoly. The unity that he must promote is thus a unity in plurality. And naturally, the shepherd himself must not become a cause of division in the community.

This service of unity goes beyond his own flock. The priest must meditate on Jesus' words that there are other sheep that do not belong to his sheepfold; he must lead these too, so that finally there is only one shepherd and one flock (John 10:16). And he will make his own the prayer that Jesus addressed to his Father on the eve of his death, the prayer he has left us as his testament: "That they may all be one" (John 17:21).

The ecumenical dimension finds its perfect expression in this prayer, and this is why ecumenism will primarily be a spiritual matter. It takes the path of conversion, renewal, and sanctification. Prayer for unity is the soul of the entire ecumenical movement (*Unitatis Redintegratio* 8). Since it goes back to the testimony of Jesus himself, ecumenism is not a minor pastoral sideshow nor a luxury in which one can indulge after all the "real" pastoral work has been done. It is an essential part of the ministry to which priests are ordained. Ecumenism is one of the major "building sites" of the church, where the future of the church is at stake. Naturally, this building will collapse if it is not constructed on the firm foundations of the truth in love (Eph 4:15).

The First Letter of Peter contains an exhortation that I have already quoted: "Tend the flock of God that is in your charge, exercising the oversight, not under compulsion but willingly, as God would have you do it—not for sordid gain but eagerly. Do not lord it over those in your charge, but be examples to the flock" (5:2f.). According to this penetrating description of the pastoral obligations of the priest, his ministry as shepherd must not be tainted in any way by arrogance. The days of high-handed clergy are surely past (and we may add, thank God). Although priests do not stand on the lowest rung of society, they have certainly lost their place on the uppermost rung, and we need not lament this change, for precisely this was the fate of Jesus himself and of the apostle Paul (1 Cor 4:9-13; 2 Cor 4:7-15). That was why Blessed Charles de Foucauld consciously chose the last place for himself.

New temptations menace us, however. One modern form of the exercise of "lordship" is called bureaucratization—not only a potential danger but sadly also a reality in the German church, where the attempt is made to regulate *everything* by means of exhaustively detailed procedures. A priest who is a bureaucrat or who spends all his energies as the manager of his parish (or parishes) is just as much a distortion as a priest who exercises his authority high-handedly. An impersonal bureaucratic or technocratic exercise of the ministry leads in the last analysis to the disappearance of anything that could truly be called a *spiritual* ministry. This is because, as a shepherd, the priest must show his own face. He must assume his personal responsibility for the good of his flock and of each individual member of the community—a responsibility that cannot be delegated to anyone else. The words of Jesus must apply to the priest too: "I know my own and my own know me" (John 10:14).

Another temptation is the reduction of the priestly ministry to chairing committees. Every reasonable person knows that pastoral work entails meetings, which are often tedious. The danger is that modern Catholicism, which delights in the creation of ever more numerous committees and groups, will thereby absorb the energies of priests who are already overburdened. Too much committee work prevents the priest from doing his own pastoral work and from giving his own personal testimony, since he can hide behind the committees and the decisions that they take. This is a false pastoral modesty, which shows not strength but weakness. Jesus did not say, Form a committee. He said, Get moving and get going!

Who Is a Good Shepherd?

Can we sketch a portrait of the shepherd who takes his pastoral service and responsibility seriously? Let me mention only a few traits.

The good shepherd is one who leads and has the courage to indicate a clear and reliable direction on the basis of the faith. This is particularly necessary today, when so many are like sheep without an orientation. Vagueness and assimilation to what many people would like to hear are not a pastoral attitude but a pastoral failure. The shepherd is also one who does not react harshly and coldly, but shows understanding, compassion, and patience in his dealings with those who cannot keep up with the pace of the journey, who lag behind, and who are weak. The shepherd is one who is able to speak the truth in love.

The good shepherd is a friend of life, who opens up for others the sources of life and gives them spiritual nourishment on their journey, counseling, consoling, and encouraging them as he accompanies them on their way through life. He helps them to discover the true life, and to have this life in fullness in Jesus Christ.

The good shepherd does not spend all his time with the inner circle of those who always belong to the church anyway. He goes in search of those who have strayed, those who are lost, those who have become alienated from the church, or are on her periphery. He will rescue them from the thorny thickets in which they are entangled, even if this means that he himself gets scratched or grazed. And if they cannot yet run on their own, he will place them on his strong shoulders and bring them back home.

The good shepherd will not utter blanket accusations against the rich, but he will nevertheless have a heart for the poor, the little ones, the weak, the children, the sick, and the handicapped, for all those whose life has been blighted in some way and whose existence is marginal. He will fight for their rights and their dignity, for justice and for each one's freedom to live his own life.

The good shepherd is vigilant and alerts his flock to dangers. He defends it when dangers threaten from without or within. In difficult situations such as persecution, he does not run away. He does not try to bring his own little life into safety but stays put in danger together with the flock that has been entrusted to him.

Finally, the good shepherd will not pasture himself. He does not seek his own advantage. He does not spare himself but commits his life and gives it for others. This is why the pastoral ministry cannot be restricted to a certain number of hours in the rectory office; it demands the whole man and the whole person. In extreme situations, it can even demand that the priest lay down his life. It may be true that in our Western countries such extreme challenges and dangers do not confront us at present and seem unlikely in the near future; but there are many regions in the world where persecution and oppression are a grim reality.

Great pastoral saints can show us what all this means in practice. The church fathers were not only outstanding theologians; most of them were also bishops, and, as such, the pastors of their communities. After the Reformation, Charles Borromeo initiated a thoroughgoing pastoral renewal, while Philip Neri's apostolate on the streets and his pastoral care for neglected children made him the "second apostle of Rome." With his pastoral work among young people, based on joy and friendship, Don Bosco established new landmarks. Don Luigi Orione began pastoral work in the new suburbs of Rome and took care of "those most abandoned and furthest from God." After the collapse of the old imperial church in Vienna, Clement Mary Hofbauer took new paths in individual pastoral work and lay movements. In the period between the two world wars, Ruper Mayer in Munich and Carl Sonnenschein in Berlin were forerunners of today's "urban pastoral work." And we give thanks to God for the many holy pastors who carry out their ministry today.

I am convinced that there are many young men who see this pastoral ministry as a challenge and a vocation, and who are generous enough to say their *Adsum,* "Here I am—I am ready!" But they will not be led to take this step by a watered-down picture of the priesthood. The power of conviction lies only in the example of a priest who lives his ministry one hundred percent.

– 6 –

The Priest as a Witness to the Gospel

Evangelization: The Identity of the Church

In the upheavals of the last decades, many well-proven methods in pastoral work were examined afresh. They turned out to be blunted: most people today can no longer be reached with these methods. Where were we to find new methods? The attempt was made to learn from psychological and didactic methodologies, from modern methods of communication, and even from economic marketing strategies. After all, the children of this age are often more shrewd than the children of light (Luke 16:8), so why not learn from them? In general, however, this has not taken us very far. Investigations of this kind can certainly *help* us in our pastoral work, but they cannot give us the orientation we need. For that, we must take

Jesus and the apostles as our teachers. And their lesson is unambiguous: they see preaching, or more precisely missionary preaching, as the primary task. This remains true today.

Jesus understands himself as the messenger of joy whom the prophet had foretold (Isa 52:7). The evangelist Mark summarizes Jesus' message as follows: "He proclaimed the Gospel of God and said, 'The time is fulfilled, and the kingdom of God has come near; repent, and believe in the Gospel'" (1:15). According to Luke, Jesus quotes from the prophet Isaiah (61:1f.) in his first sermon in Nazareth: "The Spirit of the Lord is upon me, because he has anointed me to bring good news [*euangelizein*] to the poor" (Luke 4:18). During his earthly ministry, Jesus worked by means of his words and by means of the miracles that confirmed his words. We are told: "He went about among the villages teaching [*didaskein*]" (Mark 6:6). This is why he was considered a "rabbi" (Mark 9:5; 11:21; John 1:38, etc.), though one who taught a completely new doctrine (*didachē*) with authority (*exousia*), unlike the scribes (Mark 1:22, 27).

Similarly, when Jesus sends out his disciples, the heart of his commission to them is preaching: "Go and proclaim the good news, 'The kingdom of heaven has come near'" (Matt 10:7; see Luke 9:2, 6). The three Synoptic Gospels close with this mission: "Go into all the world and proclaim the good news to the whole creation!" (Mark 16:15; cf. Matt 28:19f.; Luke 24:47; Acts 1:8).

Immediately after the coming of the Holy Spirit, the apostles began to preach with great courage and openness (Acts 2:14-36; 3:11-26; 4:8-12, etc.) and thereby spread joy everywhere (Acts 8:39; 13:48, 52; 15:3, 31). They gave this ministry of the word absolute priority over the ministry of the tables (Acts 6:2).

Paul presents himself to the community in Rome, which he does not yet know personally, as one "called to be an apostle, set apart for the gospel of God" (Rom 1:1; see Acts 9:15; 1 Thess 1:9). He goes so far as to say: "Christ did not send me to baptize but to proclaim the gospel" (1 Cor 1:17). In his Letter to the Romans, he boasts that he has preached the gospel everywhere from Jerusalem to Illyricum; now he wishes to bear witness to it in Rome too, and then to go on to Spain, that is, to the boundaries of the then known world (Rom 15:19, 23f.).

The Pastoral Letters reflect a new situation. We are only in the second generation, but the communities are already in crisis: teachers of heresy have appeared, and this has led to internal controversies. The Pastoral Letters respond to this threat by pointing to the important principle (already found in Paul: cf. 1 Cor 11:23; 15:3) that one must keep to the *paradosis,* the "tradition." They urge that instruction be given in the faith, and appeal to those in positions of responsibility to keep to the sound doctrine that has been handed down to them (1 Tim 1:10; 2 Tim 4:2f.; Titus 1:9, etc.). We read about the bishop: "He must have a firm grasp of the word that is trustworthy in accordance with the teaching, so that he may be able both to preach with sound doctrine and to refute those who contradict it" (Titus 1:9).

The admonitions are dramatic:

In the presence of God and of Christ Jesus, who is to judge the living and the dead, and in view of his appearing and his kingdom, I solemnly urge you: proclaim the message; be persistent whether the time is favorable or unfavorable; convince, rebuke, and encourage, with the utmost patience in teaching. For the time is coming when people will not put up with sound doctrine, but having itching ears, they will accumulate for themselves teachers to suit their own desires, and will turn away from listening to the truth and wander away to myths. As for you, always be sober, endure suffering, do the work of an evangelist, carry out your ministry fully. (2 Tim 4:1-5)

This makes it clear that for Jesus, the apostles, and their successors preaching and teaching are central, and that these two tasks are more important than any other. Paul says of himself: "Woe to me if I do not proclaim the gospel!" (1 Cor 9:16), and this can be applied to all his successors. Paul VI once said that the proclamation of the gospel is the true identity of the church; she exists in order to evangelize. This applies especially to bishops and priests: their primary task is the proclamation of the gospel.

already made the commitment of faith, and to offer courses of information about the faith; but it is much more important for the seeker to encounter convinced Christians who irradiate something of the fire and the joy of the Christian existence and who tell others about their experience. In western Europe, our Christian existence has become far too much of a private matter that we anxiously protect from other people's eyes. We are too shy about bearing witness.

We need to discover new forms of the popular missions that were once both common and successful. One example is the urban missions that have recently been carried out in Vienna, Paris, Lisbon, and other European cities. We must not leave this field to the Pentecostal churches, for it is not only in the Southern Hemisphere that they are booming! The experience of the World Youth Days, huge pilgrimage Masses, diocesan and national assemblies of Catholics, great jubilees and other big "events" shows how important these are in a world dominated by the mass media. They can prompt people to think about the Christian faith, and they can communicate the experience of belonging to a wide fellowship.

Naturally, however, it is only normal, regular preaching that can make a genuinely lasting impact. Today, this must be an act of evangelization with a mystagogical character. In other words, it must introduce the hearers into the mystery of faith. It must concentrate on the central points, in keeping with the hierarchy of truths (see *Uni-*

tatis Redintegratio 11). This does not make other matters redundant, but we should remember that they can be understood only on the basis of the core of the good news. Another important point: our preaching should not be *only* a list of all the things that are forbidden to Christians and society. Boundary lines, commandments, and prohibitions frighten people off and make them depressed, since the law without the grace of Christ makes excessive demands of human beings; it is the gospel that sets them free to love and to perform works of love. This is why our preaching must begin with the positive option of the faith—the inner beauty of the faith and of a life lived by faith. This is what we must emphasize, for this can inspire and fascinate our hearers.

The preaching of the faith must be accompanied by instruction in the faith. For Jesus and the apostles, preaching always involves doctrine. Faith is not some vague feeling, nor simply a matter of practicing old habits. It has specific contents that one can and should get to know. One can love only that which one knows; and when one loves, one longs to know more. This makes the holistic and organic catechumenal introduction to the practice of the faith a fundamental duty of every priest and bishop. I was particularly interested in the renewal of catechesis during my university years, and above all after I became a bishop; we had nearly finished work on a concept for this renewal, but the call to Rome meant that I did not have the opportunity to try it out in praxis.

The origins of the catechumenate go back to the New Testament (Gal 6:6); the instruction of a noble Ethiopian by Philip (Acts 8:26-40) is regarded as the earliest model of this kind of catechetical teaching, which was very important in the early church. Good examples are the *Mystagogical Catecheses* of Cyril of Jerusalem and the catechetical instruction of Saint Augustine. At the beginning of the third century, Hippolytus of Rome gives us a detailed description of this catechesis and tells us that it should take three years (*Traditio Apostolica* 17). The catechumenate was one of the strong points of the early church and has remained so in missionary churches up to the present. It is one of the basic obligations of every pastor.

Unfortunately, however, this catechetical introduction, which is not merely intellectual but embraces the whole person, is in a bad state in our part of the world. The family and the school are hardly ever able to carry out this task. The council laid down that an adult catechumenate in several stages should be reintroduced (*Sacrosanctum Concilium* 64), but there has as yet been little echo here of this forward-looking ordinance. This means that the knowledge of the faith has reached a historical low point. Christians have nothing to reply to critical objections: they cannot give an account of their faith, nor can they bear witness to it.

This makes a renewal of the catechumenate for children and young people, and the elaboration of an adult catechumenate, a very urgent pastoral task in our new missionary situation, both as a preparation for baptism and as a postbaptismal initiation into the reality of this sacrament. Family catechesis, which involves parents in the preparation of their children for first confession and first communion, has already proved very valuable. Another positive sign is that many laypeople, some already elderly, are studying theology. This represents a potential that can bear great fruit in the pastoral field.

The Word of God—Light of Life and Light of the World

We frequently hear the complaint that it is not easy for the Word of God to attract attention and win a hearing in a world that is subjected to a constant stream of words and images. This is certainly true, and it causes many pastors sleepless nights. Often, one must wait through a long winter until spring comes and the seed sown in the fall begins to sprout. In this context, the parable of the sower is very realistic: seed falls along the path, on stony ground, or among the thorns, but there is also seed that falls on good soil and bears a rich harvest (Matt 13:1-9 par.). The early church saw how the Word of God "ran" and spread like wildfire (2 Thess 3:1), for the simple reason that it is not trivial chatter but gives the answer to the deepest questions and yearnings that are etched on human hearts.

The Word of God is not primarily a word or a doctrine *about* God, but the word that God himself addresses to us in the most personal manner. When we speak of the Word of God, we affirm that God is not like the "dumb idols" (1 Cor 12:2) "who have mouths but do not speak" (Ps 115:5). In the Old Testament, God reveals himself as the God who exists, who is with us, and is on our side (Exod 3:12, 14f.). The God of the Old and New Testaments is a God who speaks, a living God who addresses human beings in love and speaks to us as to friends (Exod 33:11; John 15:14f.).

The fact that God is a God who speaks means that the ultimate horizon of life and of the world is not some mute law of nature, some anonymous fate or sheer meaninglessness, but One who is on our side and who addresses us personally. God says, It is my will that you exist; I have written you on my hand (cf. Isa 49:16). I wish to draw you to my heart and welcome you into fellowship with myself.

In the New Testament, we find the full revelation of the God who is love (1 John 4:8, 16). The knowledge that I am kept safe in God's love takes away fear and uncertainty, the feeling of abandonment, and the unfathomability of our existence. Through this knowledge, life becomes meaningful and secure. To preach the Word of God is therefore to give people dignity and security, meaningfulness and consolation. The Word of God gives us happiness and a joyful heart (Jer 15:16). To preach this

Word is to communicate to people joy in God and joy in the fact that they themselves exist.

We find the most detailed reflections on the power of God's Word to reach human hearts in the Gospel of John. In the prologue (John 1:1-12), the Gospel looks back to the Book of Genesis: "He spoke . . . and it came to be" (Gen 1:3, etc.). Everything that exists came into being through the Word of God (cf. Heb 1:3). Accordingly, the Word of God does not come to us as something alien and external. It is not like a mantle that is thrown over us from without. It comes "into that which is its own." It is the light that has given light to every human being from the beginning of time. It is the light of human beings, enlightening them and making them shine; it is both light and life.

Naturally, the Johannine prologue is aware that this light is not accepted by human beings. They suppress it, and this is why the world has grown dark. The struggle between light and darkness, truth and falsehood, runs through the whole of history and characterizes our own days too. When we contemplate this struggle, which is as old as humankind, we can understand the liberating quality of Jesus' words: "I am the light of the world. Whoever follows me will never walk in darkness, but will have the light of life" (John 8:12). The good news about Jesus Christ reveals the human person to his own self and gives him light for the path of life.

It is the task of preaching to spread the light of life in

the darkness of the world, to bring light into human lives, and to reveal the true meaning of created things and of life itself. The preacher is not imposing some ideology on his hearers, an abstract doctrine or moral code that is irrelevant to life. His task is to bring light into their lives and to interpret their experiences by showing what these truly mean. This is a vital pastoral service in support of *life*, so that people may have life to the full (cf. John 10:10). Understood in this way, the gospel is the good news that makes life bright and joyful. It can be a light to our feet on the dark paths of life (Ps 119:105).

What we preach is not "the Christian worldview." Our goal is to enkindle faith, hope, and love—a goal that Saint Augustine so brilliantly describes when he asks, What does it mean to believe in God? His answer runs as follows: "To be devoted to him by faith, to love him by faith, to turn to him by faith and to be united to those who are his members" (*In Ioannem* 29.6).

There have always been great preachers whose words not only instructed their hearers but also moved them, stirred them up, inspired them, and consoled them. Almost all the church fathers were great preachers. It suffices to recall John Chrysostom and Augustine of Hippo; medieval examples are Bernard of Clairvaux and Dominic, with his Order of Preachers. There were also great mystical preachers, such as Master Eckhart and John Tauler and Anthony of Padua in the Middle Ages. In more recent centuries, we have Abraham a Santa Clara,

Jacques-Bénigne Bossuet, Michael Sailer, John Henry Newman, Bishop Paul Wilhelm Keppler, and many others. In Nazi Germany, the sermons of Blessed Clement Augustus von Galen, the "Lion of Münster" (and later cardinal), woke many people up to the reality of the situation. In my student days in Munich, I saw how people streamed into St. Ludwig's church to hear the sermons of Romano Guardini. The living word may seem weak, but when it is filled with the Spirit, it can become immensely powerful, touching hearts and kindling a fire.

"Working for the Gospel as a Priest"

The Word of God does not give us value-free, neutral information. Nor does it tell us harmless little anecdotes or a story about other people. It touches our very heart and brings about what it says. It purifies (John 15:3); it is "the power of God" that brings salvation to all who accept it (Rom 1:16; Eph 1:13). The Letter to the Hebrews states this very clearly: "The Word of God is living and active, sharper than any two-edged sword, piercing until it divides soul from spirit, joints from marrow; it is able to judge the thoughts and intentions of the heart. And before him no creature is hidden, but all are naked and laid bare to the eyes of the one to whom we must render an account" (4:12f.). The "Word of God" is *nomen actionis,* the designation of an *action,* a performative word (*verbum efficax*). It has a quasi-sacramental power.

Paul understands his ministry of preaching as a liturgical service. He speaks of a spiritual worship (*latreuein*, Rom 1:9) and of a priestly service. He calls himself a celebrant of the liturgy (*leitourgos*) who works for the gospel as a priest (*hierourgein*) in order to make ready the Gentiles as a sacrificial gift (*prosphora*) that is pleasing to God (Rom 15:16). When he describes his apostolic ministry of preaching the gospel, therefore, Paul has recourse to priestly and liturgical terminology. Through his preaching, he wishes to spread the pleasant fragrance of the gospel to the praise and glory of God (2 Cor 2:15). In another passage, he writes that he wishes to "be poured out as a libation over the sacrifice and the offering of your faith" (Phil 2:17).

In the classical period, the word *liturgy* referred to a public service. This means that Paul understands his preaching not as a personal charismatic undertaking of his own, but as a public and official service carried out by an apostle who has divine authorization. Even today, apostolic authorization is required for preaching in the celebration of the eucharist: this is first of all the task of the bishop, and then of the priests and deacons to whom he entrusts this work.

As liturgy, the ministry of the Word of God has nothing in common with propaganda (whether secular, religious, or philosophical); its mission is neither social nor political, nor does it promote an ideology. Paul warns against false intentions here: he emphasizes that he does not preach the Word of God for financial gain (2 Cor 2:17; cf. Phil 1:15-17). For him, this Word is "the word about the cross" (1 Cor 1:18); in his preaching, all that he seeks to know is Jesus Christ crucified. He knows that the proclamation of the crucified Christ is folly in the eyes of the world, but God's power and wisdom for the one who believes (1 Cor 1:23f.). Thus, he is not interested in brilliant speeches and scholarly wisdom, nor in eloquent and prudent words. The wisdom that interests Paul is not the wisdom of this world, but that of God. In his preaching, the mystery of God's hidden wisdom is to be revealed, namely, the great things that God has in store for those who love him (1 Cor 2:1-9).

The preaching of God's wisdom opens up new horizons and gives deeper insight. Paul uses language that evokes liturgical hymns when he speaks of the eternal mystery and plan of salvation that encompasses the entire world (Rom 16:25-27; Eph 1:3-14; cf. Eph 3:4f., 9; Col 1:26; 1 Pet 1:20). Ultimately, this mystery of salvation will find its accomplishment in the new heaven and the new earth, which only God can create (Isa 65:17; 2 Pet 3:13; Rev 21:1). This makes the ministry of the world a ministry of hope, and this is very necessary today, for it is only this hope that makes human life possible. Irenaeus of Lyons summarized this in the wonderful affirmation, "The glory of God is the living human being" (*Adversus haereses* 4.20.7).

"You Will Be My Witnesses"

Preaching will always be very important, and must be prepared with care; but the proclamation of the Word of
God is a many-faceted phenomenon that also includes
catechesis, that is, the basic and complete initiation into
the faith and the life of the church, and other forms of
instruction in the faith. Every pastoral conversation (even
chance encounters), all encouragement, exhortation, and
consolation can bear testimony to the faith.

All these various forms of proclamation have one thing
in common: proclamation is testimony, and the one who
proclaims is a witness. This testimony is first and foremost the testimony of one's life: the ministry of proclamation is a ministry of witnessing that requires personal
commitment on the part of the one who exercises it.
Thomas Aquinas defines preaching as *contemplata tradere*,
that is, handing on to others what has first passed
through one's own contemplation and one's own life. A
witness speaks not only with his mouth but with his
whole person. He vouches personally for the truth to
which he bears witness, and he defends it fearlessly, even
if this should cost his life. When Saint Walter disputed
with King Philip I of France, he told him, "It is better to
suffer death for the truth than to yield disgracefully to
falsehood!"

Jesus himself is the faithful witness (Rev 1:5; 3:14)

who came into the world to bear witness to the truth (John 18:37; cf. I Tim 6:13). Before his ascension, he told his disciples: "You will be my witnesses . . . to the ends of the earth" (Acts 1:8). Paul was appointed a witness (*martys*) on the road to Damascus (Acts 22:15; 26:16), and such a testimony can lead to death in times of persecution. Jesus told his disciples that they would be dragged before governors and courts, where they would have to bear witness (Mark 13:9; Matt 10:18; Luke 21:13f.).

The first to put the seal of his blood to his testimony was the martyr Stephen (Acts 22:20; cf. 7:54-60). All the apostles took the same path, and the Revelation of John tells us that countless other witnesses were slain because they had borne witness to Jesus (Rev 6:6). But their defeat was only apparent: it was in reality they who defeated the adversary "through the blood of the Lamb and through the word of their testimony" (Rev 12:11).

Many bishops and priests suffered martyrdom as witnesses to Jesus Christ in the early centuries—the martyr popes of the early days, great bishops and theologians such as Ignatius of Antioch, Polycarp, Irenaeus of Lyons, Cyprian, and many others whose names are recorded in the church's martyrology and whose memory is kept alive in the liturgy. Many later periods of church history were also times of martyrdom, and very many missionaries died. In my own country, we venerate above all the apostle of the Germans, Saint Boniface; in Japan, Paul Miki and his companions are venerated; in Africa, the Ugandan martyrs. These are only a few examples; many other names could be mentioned.

No other century had as many martyrs as the twentieth century—under National Socialism and Communism, in the Soviet Union and in China, in Spain and Mexico and in the Third World. Innumerable priests were killed or suffered unspeakable torments in prisons, concentration camps, and labor camps. We must look to these martyrs and confessors from the immediate past with great reverence. We can find inspiration in exemplary priests such as Maximilian Kolbe, Bernard Lichtenberg, Rupert Mayer, Joseph Metzger, and many others; and we should not forget the martyrs of other churches, such as Dietrich Bonhoeffer in Germany. All these witnesses give us good reasons for hope, since we are entitled to believe that the blood of these martyrs in the last century will be the seed of new Christians in the twenty-first (see Tertullian, *Apologeticum* 50.14).

Minister of Reconciliation

Proclaiming God's Abundant Mercy

When I was a young priest, I spent many hours in the confessional every Saturday. Sometimes, I spent the entire day in the confessional before great feast days. Sometimes this was laborious; sometimes it was a matter of routine; but in no other situation did I acquire so much pastoral experience at the beginning of my ministry. Even after only a short time, hearing confessions changed the style of my sermons—and it changed me too. The most important thing I learned was how wonderful it is to be permitted to tell other people of God's abundant and inexhaustible mercy and to assure them that he is always ready to forgive. This brought consolation and joy into the darkness that reigned in many people's lives.

Mercy and forgiveness are key words in the Bible. They are central to the Old Testament, where only a superficial reading can see God as a God of anger and vengeance. In one very early text, we read: "The Lord, the Lord, a God merciful and gracious, slow to anger, and abounding in steadfast love and faithfulness" (Exod 34:6f.).

The most moving passage is in the prophet Hosea, where God forgives his faithless bride, Israel: "How can I give you up, Ephraim? How can I hand you over, O Israel? . . . My heart recoils within me; my compassion grows warm and tender. I will not execute my fierce anger; I will not again destroy Ephraim; for I am God and no mortal, the Holy One in your midst, and I will not come in wrath" (11:8f.). The Psalms often speak of forgiveness (Ps 25:18; 32:1; 51; 65:3; 79:9), and one prayer breaks out in a hymn of praise: "Bless the Lord, O my soul, and do not forget all his benefits—who forgives all your iniquity, who heals all your diseases" (Ps 103:2f.).

The Old Testament envisages a ritual communication of forgiveness, especially by means of the annual celebration of the great Day of Atonement (*Yom Kippur*, Lev 16). We also read of intercession for others, so that their sins may be forgiven: Abraham prays for the men of Sodom (Gen 18:22-33), and Moses prays for the sins of the people (Exod 32:11-13). The fourth Song of the Servant of the Lord goes one decisive step further, when it says that he takes upon himself the sins of the people: he bears these sins and prays for the guilty (Isa 53:4, 7, 11f.).

The public ministry and the message of Jesus are in

continuity with the Old Testament, but also go beyond it. In his first great sermon in the synagogue in Nazareth, Jesus says that he has been sent to proclaim a year of the Lord's grace (Luke 4:19). This is no "cheap grace" (to borrow Bonhoeffer's phrase), since Jesus began his public ministry by submitting on our behalf to the penitential baptism of John (Mark 1:9-11), and there is an indissoluble link in his teaching between the message of the grace of forgiveness and the appeal "Repent!" (*metanoeite,* Mark 1:15 par.; Luke 13:1-5, etc.)—the same link that is already present in the prophets. Forgiveness cannot be detached from the demand "Do not sin any more!" (John 5:14; 8:11). Jesus warns that those who refuse to repent will face judgment (Matt 10:15; 11:22, 24; 21:33-44; 22:1-14). It is impossible to interpret his teaching in such a way that we could excise this threat of judgment.

The central element of his message is, however, the mercy of God, who is always ready to forgive. This is lived out in Jesus' own conduct toward sinners. He calls them to follow him (like Levi, the tax collector [Mark 2:13-17 par.]), and he scandalizes his enemies by inviting them to eat with him (Mark 2:16; Matt 11:19; Luke 15:1f.). We find the most impressive presentation of his message in the parables of the lost sheep, the lost drachma, and above all the prodigal son (Luke 15). It would be better to call this the parable of the forgiving father. It made a profound impression on those who first heard it, and on all who have read it since.

Jesus' conduct and message were inevitably a provocation to the self-righteous, and the provocation was complete when he told them, "Those who are well have no need of a physician, but those who are sick; I have come to call not the righteous but sinners" (Mark 2:17). "There will be more joy in heaven over one sinner who repents than over ninety-nine righteous persons who need no repentance" (Luke 15:7).

Jesus went one step further. Not only did he proclaim God's forgiveness; he himself forgave. "Your sins are forgiven" (Mark 2:5). The scribes of that period could not fail to regard this as blasphemy, and they asked, "Who can forgive sins but God alone?" (2:7). They had correctly perceived what was at stake here. Jesus' conduct toward sinners and his forgiveness of sins are an implicit claim to do something that only God can do, and this is what Jesus means when he tells the parable of the prodigal son: *my* conduct shows you *God's* conduct. I am acting in the place of God. This is nothing less than the claim to be the Son of God.

Jesus' conduct, which outraged the scribes, and his message about God's mercy toward sinners led to his condemnation. His death seemed to be God's judgment; indeed, it seemed that he was accursed, for scripture says that a hanged man is under God's curse (Deut 21:23; Gal 3:13). The early church refused to let its faith be shaken by this objection. It agreed that Jesus' death was God's

Jesus' conduct toward sinners and his forgiveness of sins are an implicit claim to do something that only God can do, and this is what Jesus means when he tells the parable of the prodigal son: my conduct shows you God's *conduct.*

judgment of sin; but this was the judgment of *our* sins:
Jesus' death was seen as a vicarious death "for the many."
We find this interpretation in one of the oldest pieces of
tradition in the New Testament: "Christ died for our sins
in accordance with the scripture" (I Cor 15:3; cf. 11:24).
And so the grace of forgiveness is no cheap grace: it was
purchased at a high price, "with the precious blood of
Christ" (I Pet 1:18; I Cor 6:20).

Paul developed and deepened this interpretation (Rom
5:6-11, etc.). He can write, "For our sake, God made him
to be sin who knew no sin, so that in him we might
become the righteousness of God" (2 Cor 5:21; cf. Gal
3:13). A marvelous exchange has taken place: he who is
sinless and righteous is made a sinner, in order that we
sinners might become righteous. Many of the classic Pas-
siontide hymns, such as the medieval *Salve, caput cruentatum*
("O sacred head, sore wounded"), are meditations on
Paul's paradoxical affirmation.

The Letter to the Hebrews integrates this message into
its high-priestly theology and finds penetrating words to
express it: "We do not have a high priest who is unable to
sympathize [*sympathein*] with our weaknesses, but we have
one who in every respect has been tested as we are, yet
without sin. Let us therefore approach the throne of
grace with boldness, so that we may receive mercy and
find grace to help in time of need" (4:15f.; cf. 7:25-28).
The author adds that Jesus' gift of his own life for us

continues, in the sense that he is the perfect high priest who has been exalted to the right hand of God and lives forever to make intercession for us (7:25; 9:24).

This is why the Christian, and especially the priest, must be able to sympathize with others, above all with the weak and sinners; empathy and imagination are required. *Sympathein*—sympathy and empathy—is not at all the same as a falsely liberal attitude that makes endless concessions to human weakness: we must love the sinner, not the sin. There is nothing in a priest that people find so repellent as hard-heartedness, where they look to find mercy. They resent this, and it is not quickly forgotten! In the Sermon on the Mount, Jesus praises the merciful (Matt 5:7), and he esteems mercy more highly than any sacrifice (Matt 9:13; 12:7). Indeed, the Letter of James can say, "Judgment will be without mercy to anyone who has shown no mercy; but mercy triumphs over judgment" (2:13).

The perspective of mercy is one of the fundamental principles guiding the application of canon law. A legal decision must not only be formally just; it must also be equitable, that is, appropriate to the personal situation of the person involved (*aequitas canonica*), and this is why the highest principle of the application of church law is the salvation of souls (Code of Canon Law, can. 1752). Thomas Aquinas wrote as follows: "Justice without mercy is cruelty; mercy without justice means the dissolution of all right order" (*Commentary on Matthew* 5.7.74).

"Your Sins Are Forgiven"

In Acts, we see how the apostles faithfully continued after
Easter to preach Jesus' message about the forgiveness of
sins (2:38; 5:31; 10:43; 13:38; 26:18). The New Testament church was convinced that the forgiveness of sins is
bestowed through baptism (Acts 2:38; Rom 6:1-11, etc.).
The question soon arose, however: What happens when a
baptized person lapses back into sin? This was not merely
a matter of theory. The sad experience of the early
church, where so many communities failed to live up to
their calling, has left its mark on the lists of vices in the
Letters of Paul (Gal 5:19-21, etc.), who often rebukes
them for their quarrels and their lack of love (1 Cor 3:3f.;
11:18-22).

The Letter to the Hebrews appears to exclude the possibility of a second repentance (Heb 6:4-6; 10:26-31),
and this led to vehement controversies in the postapostolic period. Against rigorist tendencies, the church
decided in favor of the path of mercy, which meant that
a second repentance was possible. This was regarded as a
laborious second baptism, or as a second plank of rescue
after the shipwreck of sin (Tertullian, *De paenitentia* 7; 12).

The decisive question then and now is: Did Jesus really
give his disciples the authority to forgive sins? Have we as
priests the right to say, "Your sins are forgiven"? Jesus does
not mention this explicitly when he sends out the disci-

ples; it is his words about binding and loosing that show us the answer to this question. "Truly I tell you, whatever you bind on earth will be bound in heaven, and whatever you loose on earth will be loosed in heaven" (Matt 18:18). In another passage, the same words are employed to bestow in a special way on the apostle Peter the authority that all the disciples receive here (cf. Matt 16:19), but there is no contradiction between the two texts, since the "community rule" (18:15-20) gives to the communities (i.e., the local churches) the same authority that is given to Peter in the context of the universal church.

In rabbinical Judaism, the authority to "bind and loose" refers both to teaching and to discipline. The rabbi can make decisions about the interpretation of the Torah, which are also disciplinary decisions that "bind"—in other words, they exclude someone from the fellowship. This exclusion can later be "loosed"—that is, the person is reintegrated into the fellowship.

Matt 18:18, in the "community rule," clearly emphasizes the disciplinary aspect. At the same time, however, the disciplinary act of exclusion or of reintegration is valid "in heaven," that is, in the eyes of God; and this goes beyond the purely disciplinary level. Reintegration into the fellowship, after the exclusion provoked by sin, is also reintegration into fellowship with God. In later terminology, we could say that the exclusion and the reintegration have a sacramental meaning. Reconciliation with the community is also reconciliation with God.

The Fourth Gospel confirms this interpretation. We find a variant on Matt 18:18 in the account of the appearance of the risen Jesus to his disciples. He breathes on them and says, "Receive the Holy Spirit. If you forgive the sins of any, they are forgiven them; if you retain the sins of any, they are retained" (John 20:23). The authority to forgive or retain sins is the paschal gift of Jesus to his disciples.

We find already in the New Testament the basic structure of the sacrament of penance in the form of excommunication and reconciliation. Paul commands that those who have committed grave sins be excluded from the community "in the name of Jesus our Lord" (1 Cor 5:1-5; cf. 1 Tim 1:20; 2 Thess 3:6, 14f.; Titus 3:10); but if the one who is punished in this way subsequently repents, a spirit of mildness should prevail, and the sinner is to be pardoned (2 Cor 2:5-11). We also hear of the "confession" of sins (*exomologēsis*) at an early date (James 5:16; *Didache* 4.14; 14.1; *Barnabas* 19.12; *1 Clement* 51.3). The basic elements of the sacrament of reconciliation are thus present early on, even if this sacrament was often to change its concrete form in the course of church history.

It is undergoing remarkable changes today too, with the rediscovery of many forms of penance and of the forgiveness of our everyday sins: the petition "Forgive us our sins . . ."; intercessory prayer for and by others; retreats in which one examines one's life before God; conversations with a fellow Christian; and fraternal correction. . . . Many

prefer to confess their sins in the form of a detailed conversation. Nevertheless, we cannot close our eyes to the
fact that many Christians, including many priests, no
longer value the paschal gift of Jesus. The wide-scale disappearance of the sacrament of confession is one of the
most disturbing deficiencies of the contemporary church.

There are many reasons for this development. We are
often told that bad experiences in the confessional are to
blame, though it is surely fair to point out that most
middle-aged and younger Catholics have never had *bad*
experiences of this kind, for the simple reason that they
have never had *any* experience of the sacrament. Sin and
guilt are often defined today in purely legal terms, or
interpreted sociologically, psychologically, or even patho-
logically; the therapist has often taken the place of the
father confessor. In many cases, a good therapist can
help. But no therapist can say, "Your sins are forgiven."
When we look on a deeper level, we can see that the
decline of the sacrament of penance is owing to a decline
of faith. One who becomes aware of the love of God
will also become painfully aware of how little he or she
truly responds to this love. But since we know that there
is forgiveness of sins, we can admit to our failures. We
need not suppress our guilt or imagine that we ourselves
are innocent. We need not locate guilt only in the "others" or the "system," for that is mere self-righteousness.

The confession of guilt entails shame, but it is at the
same time a confession of God's grace, which is always

greater than our sin. There is a tremendous consolation and liberation in the encounter with the Lord whose mercy I am permitted to experience again and again in such a personal way. This is not an oppressive experience: it fills us with gratitude and joy. A ray falls into our hearts from the joy felt in heaven when a sinner repents.

As priests, we must ensure that we do not water down Jesus' message of divine grace. The paschal gift of the sacrament of penance is not to be squandered in the form of "cheap grace." We should reflect on the fact that the patron saint of parish priests, John Vianney, took over a parish that had gone to the dogs and no longer deserved the name of Christian. He renewed his flock through his ministry in the confessional. Other saintly priests such as Clement Mary Hofbauer and Padre Pio in San Giovanni Rotondo exercised a very fruitful ministry by hearing confessions and made a new beginning possible for many whose lives had gone off the rails. There is no other path to renewal than the path of repentance and forgiveness.

It is good to see the rediscovery of this sacrament in many places, for example at pilgrimage shrines or at the World Youth Days. This is a sign of hope and should also be a spur to concrete action. It is good for every Christian, and especially every priest, to receive the sacrament of reconciliation at set intervals, above all in Advent and Lent, which are the church's penitential seasons. This does not oppress us; it sets us free. And the regular reception of the sacrament of penance leads to new joy in the faith.

Reconciliation: A Universal Charge

Paul says that he has been entrusted with the "ministry of reconciliation" (*diakonia tēs katallagēs*, 2 Cor 5:18). The starting point and foundation of his grandiose, all-embracing theological vision is the work of reconciliation that God has accomplished through Christ. For it is not we who have reconciled ourselves to God; rather, he has reconciled himself to us through the death of his Son (Rom 5:10f.). We were once God's enemies, but now we are reconciled to him (Rom 5:10): we are a new creation (2 Cor 5:17).

This work of reconciliation has taken place once and for all, but it must be made effective in the course of history. This is why God has instituted the ministry of reconciliation and has entrusted to it the "word of reconciliation" (*logos tēs katallagēs*). The apostle does not speak this word in his own name; he speaks as one sent "in the place of Christ" as a minister of reconciliation. "God is making his appeal through us; we entreat you on behalf of Christ, be reconciled to God" (2 Cor 5:20). God alone is the source of reconciliation; and when we receive this gift, it motivates us to seek reconciliation with other people. Christ "died for all, so that those who live might live no longer for themselves, but for him who died and was raised for them" (2 Cor 5:15).

Paul goes even further. He opens up a universal, cosmic

perspective by speaking not only of our reconciliation but of the reconciliation of the world: God has reconciled the world (*kosmos*) to himself. In other letters, Paul links the message of the reconciliation of the world to the idea of a peace that embraces everyone and everything (Col 1:20; see Eph 1:10; 2:16; 6:15). One fundamental aspect is the healing of the primal fissure that runs through humankind, thanks to the peace between Jews and Gentiles (Eph 2:11-22).

This makes the priestly ministry of reconciliation relevant to much more than the individual, personal, and ecclesial dimensions: it is at the service of universal peace (*shalom*). Peace with God means that we have peace with our own selves and with our neighbor; it means peace between peoples, cultures, and religions, and peace with nature. Reconciliation and salvation are understood here in a comprehensive sense.

The affirmation that the priestly ministry of reconciliation is also at the service of reconciliation and peace in the world does not mean a new clericalism. On the contrary, a blurring of the boundaries between church and state has never been a good thing for the church, and she has usually paid a high price in the long term for the supposed privileges. Jesus drew a clear distinction between our obligations to Caesar and to God (Mark 12:14), and this means that we may not pervert the gospel into a political ideology. The priest does not employ the means of the world in his service of the world, nor are his instruments those of the political sphere. He should be a sign that protects the transcendence of the human person, and this means that he must take care not to infringe the legitimate autonomy of the political realm (*Gaudium et Spes* 36; 76).

Politics needs a societal orientation in the form of values; politics lives in fact on the basis of presuppositions that it itself cannot supply. When there are no longer any fundamental values that are binding on all in society, the resulting crisis leads ultimately to disintegration. This is why the priest performs his political service (in the broadest sense of this word) by raising his voice in support of the basic values governing life in society: the right to life, the values associated with the family, freedom, justice, solidarity, and peace. Above all, he must raise his voice on behalf of those who have no voice.

In this ministry of reconciliation, we can look to great exemplary figures such as the church fathers Athanasius and Ambrose, who criticized the policies of the emperor and laid the foundations of Christian freedom. Peter Claver opposed the slave trade and committed himself to help African slaves; Turibius of Mongrovejo and Bartolomé de las Casas defended the rights of the Amerindians. In the nineteenth century, Bishop Wilhelm Emmanuel von Ketteler was one of the first to take up social questions; he traveled to the First Vatican Council with Karl Marx's *Das Kapital* in his luggage. Blessed Adolf Kolping, "the apprentices' father," worked to help young people in their difficulties and to promote family life. In our own days, Archbishop Oscar Romero paid with his life for his commitment to the poor in Latin America. All these are models for the priest as he seeks to carry out the charge laid upon him, namely, to work on behalf of life, justice, and reconciliation.

– 8 –

Eucharistic Existence

Jesus' Great Inheritance

Pastoral care, the ministry of preaching, the ministry of reconciliation—all this is certainly very important and must never be neglected. And yet, the primary association of the priesthood, both in the consciousness of the Christian people and in the self-understanding of the priest himself, is with the eucharist. It is here that all the other tasks find their unity. Here, according to the Catholic understanding of the priesthood, is the heart of the life and work of the priest. The rhythm of his life finds its essential structure in his celebration of the eucharist on Sunday, the Lord's day, and wherever possible with a smaller group of persons every day. I find both these forms of celebration immensely valuable; each is a great gift of God.

Why do we priests do this? The answer is very simple and lies in the commission that Jesus gave the twelve at the Last Supper (Mark 14:17; Matt 26:20). In his account, Luke calls them "apostles" (22:14). Jesus said, "Do this in memory of me" (1 Cor 11:24; Luke 22:19). This authorization to consecrate bread and wine is significant, indeed astounding, but the words of institution are more than this, and they must be understood in the larger context of Jesus' public ministry as a whole.

Jesus often ate with his disciples, as well as with people who were regarded as marginal figures, "sinners." These were not just meals where people satisfied their hunger. They were intimately connected to Jesus' message about the coming of the kingdom of God (Mark 1:14). His meals were an anticipation of the promised eschatological meal in the new age (Mark 2:15f.; Luke 15:1; 19:5, etc.).

His last meal, however, was not a "meal with sinners"; only the twelve were present. It differed in other respects too from the previous meals. The exegetes debate a number of details, but we may safely assume that Jesus' last meal was a Passover meal (Mark 14:23-26 par.; we find a different account in John 18:28; 19:14, 31). Here, Jesus not only looks back to the Old Testament tradition of the liberation of Israel from Egypt; he also looks forward to the definitive liberation and the definitive coming of the kingdom of God. The catastrophe of Good Friday already casts a deep shadow over this meal, but Jesus also looks

ahead, beyond the violent death that awaits him, to the
final coming of God's reign: "Truly I tell you, I will never
again drink of the fruit of the vine until that day when I
drink it anew in the kingdom of God" (Mark 14:25; cf.
Matt 26:29; Luke 22:16).

In these words, Jesus sums up his whole proclamation
of the kingdom of God and sees his approaching death
in the light of the definitive coming of this kingdom.
This meal ends with the traditional hymn of praise (Matt
26:30). In the Garden of Gethsemane, Jesus is afraid, but
his fear does not overwhelm him. Even in this hour of
utter tribulation, his trust in God, his Father, and his
hope in God's faithfulness even beyond death do not
abandon him (Mark 14:32-42).

The Old Testament celebration of Passover was instituted as a memorial of the liberation from slavery in
Egypt and of the passage through the Red Sea (Exod
12:14; 13:3, 9; Deut 16:3). Now, with the words "Do this
in memory of me," Jesus institutes the memorial celebration of a new Passover, namely, the liberation of Jesus
from the bonds of death and his passage through death to
new life. This is the institution of the new covenant that
was announced by Jeremiah (31:31). The memorial of the
old covenant was to be celebrated again and again, and the
same is true of the new covenant. The Bible understands
"memory" (*anamnēsis, memoria*) not as a subjective act of
remembering but as an objective act of making present
that which is recalled, and this is what Jesus charges the

disciples to do. When Luke calls the twelve "apostles" in the context of the Last Supper (22:14), he indicates that this is an official commission that will not be given in the same way to *all* of Jesus' disciples.

John grasped very well the meaning of this event when he summarized it in the words "Having loved his own who were in the world, he loved them to the end" (13:1). "To the end" means to the uttermost point. In the Last Supper, we see the *non plus ultra* of love, a love greater than anything that can be imagined (*quo maius cogitari nequit*). "No one has greater love than this, to lay down one's life for one's friends" (John 15:13). Neither God the Father nor Jesus himself can go any further than this. When he says "This is my body for you," and "This is my blood, poured out for you," he is not giving us some *thing.* Rather, he is giving us himself. These words mean, "This is I myself for you, as the food and drink of the new and eternal life" (see John 6:35, 48f., 54, 58). The real presence of Jesus is understood here as a personal presence— and the personal presence as a real presence.

The institution of a new Passover memorial celebration is Jesus' great inheritance, his farewell gift to us. He makes *himself* an abiding gift to us, and this is why this celebration must take the form of *eucharistia,* praise and thanksgiving. And this is why we, taking up one of the fundamental words used in the narrative of the Last Supper (Mark 14:23; I Cor 11:24), are right today to speak so often of the Mass as the "eucharist." In this thanksgiving, Jesus made a synthesis of all that he had said and done, and of all that he is for us still. The celebration of the eucharist is thus the center and summit of the entire life of the post-Easter church, and the center and summit of the life and work of those who have received the charge "Do this in memory of me." The celebration of the Mass is the source of the priestly existence and the goal that gives this existence its meaning (*Lumen Gentium* 11: *Presbyterorum Ordinis* 6; 13). Accordingly, the celebration of the eucharist will renew in each priest his strength, his courage, and his joy.

Sacrament of Unity—Ministry of Unity

The early church grasped the centrality of the eucharist and obeyed the commission of Jesus: "Do this in memory of me." The first community in Jerusalem came regularly together for prayers and the breaking of bread, and Acts emphasizes that they did so with "joy" (*agalliasis*). This is a joy that looks ahead to the eschatological fulfillment in the kingdom (Acts 2:42, 46). Paul cites the tradition that had come down to him (1 Cor 11:23), and the four New Testament accounts of the Last Supper show clear traces of liturgical stylization. They testify thus not only to the supper that Jesus ate with his disciples but also to the celebration of the eucharist in various traditions in the earliest period after Easter.

It is probable that the Christians gathered from a very early date on the "day of the Lord" (Rev 1:10; *Didache* 14.1; Ignatius, *Magnesians* 9.1; see also Acts 20:7; 1 Cor 16:2) for the regular celebration of the "Lord's Supper" (1 Cor 11:20). Ignatius of Antioch writes at the beginning of the second century, "Endeavor to come together as frequently as possible to give praise in the eucharist of God" (*Ephesians* 13.1). The response of the martyrs of Abitina to their accusers is well known: "We cannot live without the day of the Lord [*sine dominica*]," that is, without the Sunday eucharist.

Paul tells us that this coming together to participate in the one bread and to drink from the one cup has a deeper ecclesial significance: "The cup of blessing that we bless, is it not a sharing in the blood of Christ? The bread that we break, is it not a sharing in the body of Christ? Because there is one bread, we who are many are one body, for we all partake of the one bread" (1 Cor 10:16f.). Through sharing in the one eucharistic Body of the Lord, the community becomes the one ecclesial body. If the church is truly to be the ecclesial body of Christ, it must therefore take part in the one eucharistic Body of the Lord.

These words from 1 Corinthians have made a deep impression on the church's consciousness. Already in the earliest church order, the *Didache* ("Teaching of the Twelve Apostles"), we read as follows: "As the bread was scattered on the mountains and brought together into one loaf, so may the church be gathered together from the ends of the earth into your kingdom" (9.4). Saint Augustine called the eucharist "the sacrament of unity and the bond of love" (*In Ioannem* 26.6.13). Thomas Aquinas goes so far as to say that the true *res* of the eucharist, that is, the goal which gives the sacrament its meaning, is not the real presence of the Body and Blood of Christ, since he sees this as only an intermediary reality (*res et sacramentum*). The true reality involved here is the unity of the church (*Summa theologiae* III 73.6; see *Sacrosanctum Concilium* 47; *Lumen Gentium* 3; 7; 11).

The fellowship we experience when we gather around the one table of the Lord has a deeper dimension that goes far beyond our normal meals, and this has consequences for the correct understanding of the "active participation" of the community in the celebration of the eucharist. This must mean more than an external involvement in the liturgical action, or singing and making the responses together; nor can it mean that the various functions are distributed among as many persons as possible. The Second Vatican Council speaks of a "conscious, pious, and active share in the celebration" on the part of all (*Sacrosanctum Concilium* 48; see 14; 30; 50; 114). This is to be understood as an inner participation in the liturgical action, where one commits oneself in faith to the church's fellowship.

The eucharistic understanding of *communio* has consequences above all for the way in which we understand the priestly ministry. We often speak of "presiding" at the Mass. This concept is not false, but it is superficial and invites a merely external, functional understanding of the priest's eucharistic ministry, as if he were chairing the meeting of an association. In the light of the eucharistic understanding of *communio*, the priest is not a simple president: he is the "servant of Christ and steward of God's mysteries" (I Cor 4:1). When he says the words "This is my Body," "This is my Blood," he is obviously not speaking in his own person. He is speaking and acting *in persona Christi*. It is Jesus Christ himself who speaks and acts through him (see 2 Cor 5:20; *Sacrosanctum Concilium* 33; *Presbyterorum Ordinis* 13). This is why the words of institution are linked to an epiclesis that invokes the Holy Spirit, in whom and through whom Jesus Christ acts and is present.

The eucharistic *communio* includes more than those present at any one particular liturgy. If Jesus Christ is really present in each eucharist, and there is only one Jesus Christ, then every community that celebrates the eucharist is united to every other community that does the same; no community can isolate itself from the others or from the church as a whole. The one eucharist unites all these communities into one immense, worldwide fellowship. Even a very small community in some remote spot, celebrating the eucharist in utter poverty, is not alone. It is joined in fellowship with all the other communities in the world.

This is why we mention the names of the bishop and the pope in every Mass: we wish to express thereby the fact that we are celebrating the eucharist in fellowship with the bishop and the pope, that is, in communion with the entire church. Ignatius of Antioch expresses this reality very clearly: "Let that eucharist be considered valid which is under the bishop or the one whom he charges to celebrate it" (*Smyrnaeans* 8.1). His exhortation, "Let nothing be done without the bishop!" (*Trallians* 2.1), is not an authoritarian disciplinary demand; it springs from the mystery of the one eucharist.

This makes it all the more painful that divided Christians normally cannot take part in the one table of the Lord and drink from the one chalice. We should never accept this separation at the Lord's table as if it were an unchangeable fact, since it contradicts the deepest essence of the eucharist itself. Honesty requires us to acknowledge that we cannot overcome the separation at the Lord's table without first healing the deeper roots of the schism and overcoming the differences in faith that have led to our separation into various distinct church fellowships. Eucharistic table fellowship will be honest and truthful only when we can proclaim our "Amen" together at the end of the eucharistic prayer, in the one faith that we hold with an inner conviction, acknowledging together our belief in what has just taken place on the altar in word and deed. We must work to achieve this *communio* in the one faith and the one church. We must pray for unity in order that we may celebrate this *communio* at the one table of the Lord.

Memoria Passionis—Priest under the Sign of the Cross

The background to the *communio* that we celebrate in the eucharist is an unreconciled world, and sadly also a church in which there is a great need of reconciliation. As the First Letter to the Corinthians shows, the early Christians too experienced tensions and divisions in the church and a fortiori in the world, and they were aware that these tensions and divisions reached into their own unreconciled hearts, where they inflicted deep wounds. This is why the celebration of *communio* presupposes reconciliation with one's brother (Matt 5:23f.). It is a fruit of the reconciliation bestowed on us by God (2 Cor 5:19), of the peace that Jesus Christ established on the cross (Eph 2:15f.), and of redemption through his blood (Rom 3:24; Eph 1:7). "Through his wounds we have been healed" (1 Pet 2:24).

The accounts of the Last Supper make a clear link between the cross and the eucharist. When they speak of "the blood of the covenant," they are employing sacrificial terminology (Exod 24:8; Mark 14:24), and the phrases "for you" and "for the many" express the prophetical reinterpretation of the understanding of sacrifice. The rite of breaking the bread and the affirmation that the blood is "poured out" point to the idea of sacrifice, which cannot be excised from these texts: Jesus' gift of himself and his love which goes to the uttermost point necessarily include the idea of sacrifice. The Fourth Gospel too testifies to this, when we read that water and blood flow out from the wound in Jesus' pierced side—a symbolic allusion to the sacraments of baptism and the eucharist (John 19:34). Like baptism, the eucharist has its origin in the cross: it comes forth from the open side of the Lord.

We may therefore ask how it was possible at a later date for the sacrificial character of the eucharist to be denied. This has been the object of harsh polemical debates from the Reformation period onward, but the polemic is due to the misunderstanding that to affirm the sacrificial character of the eucharist is to deny (or at least to tone down) the uniqueness and the universal character of the sacrifice that Jesus offered once and for all on the cross. The New Testament bears unambiguous witness to the uniqueness of this sacrifice (Heb 9:38; I Pet 3:18), and this is not open to discussion. Accordingly, the sacrifice of the Mass is no substitution or replacement for the sacrifice of the cross; nor is there anything "lacking" in the cross that would need to be made good by the Mass.

The solution to the problem was found through the rediscovery of what the commission "Do this in memory me" (I Cor 11:24; Luke 22:19) means. As I have said, the Bible understands the "memory" or "memorial" (*anamnēsis, memoria*) not as a subjective act of remembering but as an objective presence that is brought about by the invocation of the Holy Spirit. Accordingly, there is no repetition in the eucharist of what was done once and for all on the cross. Rather, through the church's "doing" in the Holy Spirit of the commission that has been entrusted to her, that which was done once and for all on the cross becomes really present here and now. In each eucharist, we take our place, like Mary and John, under the cross, which is present in a sacramental manner; and we also take part in the heavenly liturgy in the presence of the Lamb who was slain for us (Revelation 5-8; cf. I Pet I:19f.).

It is thus the cross transfigured by Easter that is present in the eucharistic liturgy, the cross as a sign of victory and of hope—the cross that we venerate in the liturgy on Good Friday: "We venerate your cross, O Lord, and we praise and glorify your resurrection, for behold, through the wood of the cross joy came into all the world." In his famous hymn *Vexilla Regis*, the sixth-century poet Venantius Fortunatus salutes the cross: *O crux ave, spes unica*, "Hail, O cross, our only hope!" In this way, the *memoria passionis* becomes the *memoria futuri*, the anticipatory remembrance of the glorification that still awaits us.

After all the experiences of suffering and the innumerable passion narratives of the twentieth century, we have every reason at the beginning of a new century to keep alive this understanding of the eucharist as *memoria passionis* and at the same time as a sign of hope: for without the *memoria,* the act of remembering that makes the sacrifice of the cross present, the eucharist loses its seriousness and pales into meaninglessness before the conflicts and the suffering in our world. Without the remembrance of the sacrifice of the cross, the understanding of the eucharist as a "meal" becomes superficial, vapid, and shallow. The concept of sacrifice prevents us from perverting the eucharist into a bourgeois meal that could all too easily be understood as "cheap grace." Where the eucharist is understood as *memoria passionis Christi,* it also reminds us of the passion narrative of the world. In the Book of Revelation, the homage paid to the Lamb who was slain for us includes the remembrance of all the many other persons who have been slaughtered, and in the *Agnus Dei* of the Mass we pray for mercy and peace for our whole world: "Have mercy on us. . . . Grant us peace!"

The idea of the sacrificial character of the eucharist influenced the church's language at a very early date. The *Didache* already calls the eucharist a "sacrifice" (*thysia* [14.1-3]), and Ignatius of Antioch sees the altar not merely as a table (*deipnon, mensa*) but as an altar of sacrifice (*thysiastērion* [*Magnesians* 7.2; *Romans* 2.2; *Philadelphians* 4.1 and 3, etc.]). With the development of this understanding of the eucharist, it became possible for the bishop, and later the presbyter, to be called *sacerdos.* It is wrong to criticize this development as a lapse into pagan notions of priesthood, since the decisive role here was played by the Old Testament typology that elaborates the details of the New Testament reinterpretation of priesthood—and this was now understood as a sharing in the one priesthood of Jesus Christ and as priesthood in his Spirit.

It cannot be denied that the later development was sometimes one-sided and excessively narrow; the priesthood was often reduced to the authority to say the words of consecration in the Mass. This narrow view of the link between *sacerdotium* and *sacrificium*, priesthood and sacrifice, sometimes led to an exercise of the priestly ministry that consisted *exclusively* in the celebration of the Mass, and Luther certainly had reasons for his protest. The Council of Trent, however, defended the correct Catholic understanding and initiated a reform. The fathers of Trent wanted to situate this reform within a comprehensive conception of the priesthood, but they did not succeed in doing so; it was the achievement of the Second Vatican Council to present a holistic understanding that left behind the narrow reductionisms of the past.

Naturally, this new theology does not mean a devaluation of the authority to consecrate bread and wine *in persona Christi.* On the contrary, this is a never-ceasing source of wonder and gratitude in every priest. It is simply a question of integrating this viewpoint into a more comprehensive theological and existential context, so that the entire existence of the priest can be understood as a eucharistic existence. When the priest pronounces the words "This is my Body" and "This is my Blood" *in persona Christi*, he must adopt *in propria persona* the attitude of Jesus: his existence must be wholly dedicated to God and to others, and he must make his life a sacrificial gift for God and for others. He ought to live and do what he says, and to be what he does. He ought to live the eucharist, not only celebrate it. And he ought to live it in solidarity with all those in his parish and in the whole world who are burdened down and bear the cross.

The liturgy of priestly ordination speaks unambiguously about this when it exhorts the ordinand (and reminds those already ordained): "Know what you are doing, imitate the mystery you celebrate, model your life on the mystery of the Lord's cross."

The Eucharist—Center and Summit

Many priests complain that their duties are far too numerous. They are torn between them and feel that their work almost swallows them up. In view of their excessive workload and all these obligations, they seldom succeed in organizing their lives on the basis of an inner center and in integrating the multiplicity of their tasks and commitments into a coherent whole. We must therefore ask, What is the center that gives structure and meaning

*When the priest pronounces the words "This is my
Body" and "This is my Blood"* in persona
Christi, *he must adopt* in propria persona *the
attitude of Jesus: his existence must be wholly
dedicated to God and to others, and he must make
his life a sacrificial gift for God and for others.
He ought to live and do what he says,
and to be what he does. He ought to live
the eucharist, not only celebrate it.*

to the priest's existence? The sheer number of his tasks threatens to fragment his life; that is undeniable. But we can attempt to counteract the threat of fragmentation and build up the priestly identity on the basis of the eucharist.

Theologically speaking, it is obvious that the celebration of the eucharist is the heart and center of the priest's existence, since all his other tasks either lead up to the Mass or are derived from it. Ultimately, the pastoral ministry of unity, of gathering and leading a community, means bringing people together to celebrate the eucharist. The Mass with the assembled parish is the summit and synthesis of all the tasks involved in leading a community.

The pre-eminent instrument for gathering and leading the community is the proclamation of the Word of God, which should invite and lead people to the sacraments, especially to the eucharist. Besides this, the Word itself is integrated into the celebration of the eucharist, where it takes on a particular intensity and assumes a "body." Like all the sacraments, the eucharist is a *verbum visibile,* a "word that is visible" (Augustine, *In Ioannem* 80.3), and this is why the liturgy of the Word and the homily are an integral part of the Mass. It is equally true to say that the eucharist is a form of proclamation in its own right, for Saint Paul tells us explicitly, "As often as you eat this bread and drink the cup, you proclaim the Lord's death until he comes" (I Cor 11:26).

In the Middle Ages, Thomas Aquinas showed how all the sacraments are ultimately ordered to the eucharist and form a circle around it (*Summa theologiae* III 65.3). Baptism and confirmation open the door to the eucharist; the sacrament of reconciliation, as a second and laborious baptism, welcomes the sinner back into full eucharistic fellowship. The anointing of the sick prepares those who are seriously ill or dying for participation in the fulfillment of the eucharist in the heavenly nuptial feast. Priestly ordination bestows the authority to celebrate the eucharist; the sacrament of marriage is an image of the unity and the fruitful love between Christ and the church (Eph 5:21-33) and makes the married couple and their children a kind of domestic church (*Lumen Gentium* 11).

But the celebration of the eucharist is not only a goal and center; it is also a point of departure, the source of the power to carry out our mission in the world. Just as there is a path to the eucharist from the proclamation of the Word and from the other sacraments, so too there is a path from the eucharist back out into the world. The Mass closes with the words *Ite, missa est.* Originally, this was a simple dismissal: "Go, you are dismissed"; but these words have often been understood as a reminder of our mission: *Ite, missio est,* "Go, you are sent out." The connection between worship of God and service to the world goes back to the prophets' criticism of a society that practiced splendid cultic worship but neglected social justice (Amos 5:21-27; Hos 6:6, etc.). Jesus himself took up this criticism: "I desire mercy, not sacrifice" (Matt 9:13; 12:7). Before bringing one's gift to the altar, one must first be reconciled to one's brother (Matt 5:23f.).

Even in the earliest days, therefore, the eucharistic gathering included a collection for the poor in Jerusalem (Rom 15:26-28; I Cor 16:1-4; 2 Cor 8-9, etc.). The great saints of Christian *caritas* are Nicholas of Myra, Martin of Tours, Camillus de Lellis, Elizabeth of Hungary, Vincent de Paul . . . ; the list runs down to our own days and includes figures such as Mother Teresa of Calcutta.

We cannot share the eucharistic Bread without sharing our daily bread too. Eucharistic *communio* must teach us a culture of sharing, of solidarity, and of fraternity. This is not a question of dropping a few small coins into the collection plate on Sunday! The celebration of the eucharist must be a school of love of our neighbor, of justice, and of peace. In the final analysis, the commitment of individual Christians and of the church as a whole to justice and peace has its roots in the Mass.

A eucharistic conception and concentration of the priestly ministry and of pastoral work necessarily lead us to set a clear priority. Saint Benedict said of the Divine Office: "Nothing is to be preferred to the Work of God" (*Rule,* chap. 43). We may apply this principle by analogy to the eucharist and say that it must always take priority. It must be the center and the source of meaning in our lives.

Brief Excursus on Pastoral Restructuring

In today's pastoral situation, there is a special dilemma associated with the principle of "priority for the eucharist." This priority is beautiful in theory, as everyone would admit. But in view of the shortage of priests in many parts of the world—a shortage that can now be felt in most parts of western Europe—is it realistic? How could it be put into practice? How is it possible under the present circumstances to give all Christians the genuine possibility of taking part in Sunday Mass? This question weighs heavily on the conscience of every bishop; here I speak from personal experience. There is no simple answer, but we must at least suggest a perspective for a potential future development.

One widespread answer to this question is the demand for the relaxation of the general obligation to celibacy and the admission to priestly ordination of so-called *viri probati*, men who have proved their worth in marriage and professional work. A negative answer has already been given several times to this proposal, in view of the spiritual meaning of celibacy, which has a tradition going back more than one and a half millennia and was confirmed by the Second Vatican Council. It is also doubtful whether this could really solve the problem of the shortage of priests. An exchange of priests with other countries and cultures has been recommended, and this can be a solution in some individual cases. We are grateful to many foreign priests for the excellent work they do. In many other cases, however, this has led to dubious pastoral results, and it cannot be recommended as a general solution.

In addition to emphasizing the importance of prayer for priestly vocations and to intensifying the promotion of vocations, most dioceses have begun a pastoral restructuring. Realistically speaking, and taking into account the situation in the foreseeable future, this is inevitable. In most parishes, however, there is little willingness to accept restructurings that make a profound incision into accustomed praxis in order to ensure a truly viable pastoral care for the future. This means that, alongside a number of problematic solutions, we mostly find only temporary arrangements.

One problematic attempt at a solution, which unfortunately has been implemented in many places, is to hold liturgies of the Word in parishes where the shortage of priests means that no eucharist can be celebrated; attendance at such a liturgy of the Word is considered to fulfill the Sunday obligation. This arrangement seeks to preserve as much as possible of the existing parish structures, but is not the price too high? The *structures* may be preserved, but they are deprived of the center that gives them a meaning, and thus they are hollowed out. If this praxis becomes "normal," sheer force of habit will make it the "norm" after ten or at most twenty years. The eucharist would thus have lost its central importance. It would be exchangeable with some other form of worship.

This cannot be the way ahead. It overlooks the point that the Sunday obligation is not a mere shell that can be filled with a variety of contents. This precept is the expression of the inner obligation, indeed the inner need of every Christian who is conscious of what his or her faith means, to take part on the day of the Lord, the "little Easter Sunday," in the eucharistic celebration of the death and resurrection of Jesus Christ. Liturgies of the Word on Sunday should be restricted to rare emergencies. They should not become part of normal pastoral provision.

Sometimes, Sunday Mass is dropped, not because there is no priest available but because a priest who is not the pastor of the parish—for example, a priest who is elderly but otherwise healthy, or a guest who happens to be present that day—is not permitted to celebrate the eucharist. This is completely irresponsible. It is good that laypersons are willing to accept the bishop's commission to hold liturgies of the Word on weekdays; but sometimes they claim the right to do the same on Sunday too. This is unacceptable. It means that the alleged right of individual laypersons is weightier than the eucharist, the most valuable gift that Jesus has entrusted to his church. The community has a basic *right* to the eucharist, but such a praxis subordinates this to the alleged right of individuals.

The situation is different in most dioceses, where pastoral units or federations of parishes are formed with one or more priests responsible for a number of communities. Since this kind of restructuring leaves the existing parochial structures largely intact, it does not demand that the faithful accept any abrupt changes. As long as these pastoral units do not become too large, this can be an acceptable temporary solution. With the increasing shortage of priests, however, it is more than likely that these units will in fact become too large, and no priest can be expected to shoulder such a burden in the long term—nor does it do justice to the needs of the parishes, because it means that it becomes virtually impossible for the priest to carry out pastoral work. He will be present in the parishes only for individual ministerial actions (baptisms, funerals, etc.).

We should also bear in mind that demographic changes will lead to a considerable reduction in the number of Christians in many parishes. The problem is thus not only the shortage of priests. To some extent, the shortage of the laity is already a problem, and this will get worse. This too means that in the long term, many parishes will no longer be viable. And this is why pastoral units that retain the existing parishes more or less in their present form can be only a short-term solution.

We must therefore ask what a long-term solution might look like. Or, to phrase the question more correctly: How can we shape our situation creatively, constructively, and positively, so that the *krisis* becomes a *kairos* and the eucharist retains its central position? Once again, there is no simple answer. Individual situations are so varied that no one solution can cover all of them, and we certainly cannot solve the problem by means of an ecclesiastical decree. One could however begin with pilot projects; if these were successful, they would serve as models elsewhere. We do not need to invent such projects *ex nihilo.* We can learn from the praxis of the first mission in Europe, from contemporary experiences in mission lands, and from a number of projects that have already begun in the West.

My vision or perspective on the future is the formation of spiritual centers in "midpoint churches." Most of these will be centrally situated parish churches, but they could also be monasteries or religious houses, pilgrimage shrines, or other spiritual centers. In keeping with the nature of the one eucharist, they must be places that gather the whole people of God. In other words, they must be open and attractive to all the Christians of the region.

In the midpoint churches, the faithful will not find a reduced ecclesial life that is doomed to a slow death. They will find a vibrant and full ecclesial life that includes a rich program of worship: the celebration of the eucharist, as well as the liturgy of the hours and special services for families, children, young people, and the elderly. There will also be the opportunity to confess one's sins and to receive spiritual counsel; catechesis and adult formation will be given, and those in material need will find help. Those who come to a midpoint church will experience the larger Catholic fellowship; and this will be increasingly important, since the transition from the traditional ecclesiastical structures means that practicing Christians will often lead a very isolated life in an internal or external diaspora.

A restructuring process of this kind takes a long time. This is not a path of reduction, of demolition, or of watering down, but a process of concentration that looks to the future, where the celebration of the eucharist in common is the center around which all the pastoral work of the church is focused. This would be in keeping with the sociological transition that already affects most parishes both sociologically and ecclesially. It is, of course, clear that this will involve the loss of many good traditions. But there is no point in closing our eyes to reality and continuing to hanker for a parochial life that basically belongs to the past. In most cases, the traditional territorial parish no longer corresponds to the actual geography of people's lives. We must take account of this new reality and seek to shape it actively, while we still have time.

It goes without saying that the development of midpoint churches must not mean that the surrounding ecclesiastical landscape dries out and becomes a desert. In the new missionary situation, the church must remain accessible. Accordingly, there must be many different kinds of community: house groups, prayer groups, Bible study groups, family groups, youth groups, groups based on friendship, discussion circles, and groups involved in various activities—and all these must welcome people who are seeking the truth and asking questions about religion. They should be biotopes of faith and laboratories of a new culture formed by the gospel. In this way, they can be a yeast in the world. They can also be a counterweight to the individualization and privatization of the faith. A wide field lies open here for the initiatives and activities of individual laypersons, of groups, and of movements. A pastoral unit of this new kind should be a fellowship composed of a great variety of fellowships who come together for a common celebration of the Mass on Sundays and holy days, and are sent out anew from this celebration.

This is a revival of the biblical concept of domestic churches, in a form adapted to our own situation and needs. In the early church, these domestic communities assembled around particular families, and women seem to have been the leading figures in many cases. It appears that there was a network of domestic churches in the early period, providing local support for the missionary activity of the apostle Paul (see Acts 2:46; 10:2; 21:8; Rom 16:5, 10f.; I Cor 1:16; Col 4:15; Philemon 2). Today, this idea is being renewed in many countries through the concept of "small communities," which are central to the pastoral strategies there. We find the beginnings of such a renewal in our own society too, for example where the preparation for the sacraments takes the form of family catechesis, in centers run by spiritual communities, and in the groups I have mentioned above.

The concept of midpoint churches could also meet the urgent need for a spiritual living space for priests. They should all—even those with special tasks and retired priests—be linked to the midpoint churches, since this would make it possible for the priests to have a spiritual fellowship, and perhaps (depending on the local circumstances) to have table fellowship. The team of lay fellow workers should be integrated in an appropriate way into this fellowship. There is nothing revolutionary or even new about such an idea. We find classic models in church fathers such as Basil of Caesarea and Augustine, and these could be imitated in a flexible form that meets the needs of our own days; we could also learn something from the Oratory of Philip Neri and from John Henry Newman.

This can help prevent the isolation and loneliness that afflict many priests, whose life as singles is neither meaningful nor defensible, since it is not in accord with the communal lifestyle that is an essential dimension of the fellowship of Jesus' disciples. It is vital to create new contexts for the spiritual life of priests, centered on the eucharist. Here too, we could begin with individual projects on a voluntary basis.

This is not merely a dream. I have seen such forms in countries in the Third and the First Worlds, and we must encourage and develop the seeds that are beginning to sprout in our own society too. On the basis of the celebration of the eucharist in common, such spiritual centers could have a deep influence on an entire region. This is how the first mission of Europe began, with great success. I see no other possible path for a new evangelization.

The Eschatological and Universal Cosmic Dimension

Jesus instituted the eucharist in the broad perspective of the kingdom of God (Mark 14:25 par.), and this too emphasizes the centrality of the Mass, since there is no broader perspective than this! The eucharist is thus at the very heart of what Jesus sought to do in his preaching and his public ministry, namely, to proclaim the message of the kingdom of God in which the Father will finally be "all in all" (I Cor 15:28). In the coming kingdom of God, everything will be new. God "will wipe away every tear from their eyes. Death will be no more; mourning and crying and pain will be no more." There will be "a new heaven and a new earth." God will "make all things new" (Rev 21:1-5).

The first community celebrated the breaking of the bread in common with eschatological jubilation (*agalliasis*, Acts 2:46). Indeed, Paul gives the impression that the earliest Christians worshiped with tremendous enthusiasm, and he felt obliged to intervene and tone things down (I Cor 14).

He sees the celebration of the eucharist as a "proclamation of the Lord's death until he comes" (I Cor 11:26), and this eschatological expectation found expression in the early church's liturgy in the acclamation *Maran atha*, "Our Lord comes!" (I Cor 16:22; Rev 22:20). They prayed with fervor: "Let grace come and this world pass away! *Maran atha*" (*Didache* 10.6).

In his great discourse about bread in the Fourth Gospel, Jesus calls the eucharist the bread of eternal life (John 6:35, 48f., 54, 58), bread from heaven and the food of angels (6:31, 33, 49; see Ps 78:24). Ignatius of Antioch calls it the "medicine of immortality" (*Ephesians* 20.2). It is food for the journey, a foretaste and a "pledge of future glory" (*pignus futurae gloriae,* as the antiphon at the *Magnificat* on the feast of Corpus Christi puts it). The eschatological yearning of the early church did not fall silent in later eucharistic piety. The hymn *Adoro te devote,* ascribed to Thomas Aquinas, closes with the following words: "Jesus, whom I now see veiled, I pray that my deep thirst may be quenched: that looking on you with unveiled face, I may be blessed with the sight of your glory."

The first Christians were convinced that when we celebrate the eucharist, we take part even now in the eschatological meal in the kingdom of God. This conviction is expressed most eloquently in the Letter to the Hebrews:

"You have come to Mount Zion and to the city of the living God, the heavenly Jerusalem, and to innumerable angels in festal gathering, and to the assembly of the first-born who are enrolled in heaven" (12:22f.). When we sing the threefold *Sanctus* and the *Agnus Dei* in our liturgy, or when the *Cherubic hymn* is sung in the Eastern liturgy, we unite our voices here on earth to the adoration of the Lamb in heaven (Rev 5:8-14). We join in the celebration of the celestial liturgy, and the angels and the entire company of saints celebrate with us.

Adoration is an essential dimension of the eucharist. After the council, an antithesis was often posited between eucharistic adoration and the fact that the eucharist is a meal; and one heard the objection: bread is meant to be eaten, not to be adored. The church was, of course, right at that time to prohibit the celebration of Mass before the exposed sacrament. But many people went to the opposite extreme and lost sight of the eschatological aspect of adoration. This leads to a leveling down of eucharistic piety. Fortunately, there are many signs of a rethinking here: the *stupor eucharisticus*, the "amazement" that God is truly present in our midst under the simple signs of bread and wine, is gaining ground, and there is a new appreciation of the meaning of adoration. We must learn again to pray and sing *Adoro te devote, latens Deitas*: "I adore you with devotion, O hidden Godhead."

There is a tendency in some places to give our services the form of an event or a festival, but we should take care—precisely because we live in a hectic and noisy society—to give the liturgy a meditative character which can act as a contrast to all this din. We must create spaces for silence during worship, making possible a personal encounter with God and adoration. The experience of the Taizé community shows that young people are particularly appreciative of such services.

The eschatological dimension also reveals the universal cosmic dimension of the eucharist. The entire creation is included in the eschatological kingdom of God. Bread and wine, "fruit of the earth and work of human hands," are signs that represent the cosmic dimension and make this present in the liturgy. Since they are also the product of human work and culture, these too are included in the eucharist. The transformation of bread and wine into the Body and Blood of Christ is in a certain sense an anticipation of the eschatological transfiguration and transformation of the whole of reality, both nature and culture. At the end, the whole cosmos and all that human beings have created and suffered in their lives will undergo the eschatological transfiguration. As Teilhard de Chardin said, the anticipation of the *missa coelestis* makes the eucharist *missa mundi.*

We are therefore justified in including the whole of reality, nature and culture, in the celebration of the eucharist. This is right and fitting, and absolutely appropriate. Light, colors, flowers, vestments, art, and not least music: all this should express the praise and the eschatological glorification of God. In the splendor and beauty of the liturgy, we should see at least a reflection of what will be at the end of time. The liturgy ought even now to be heaven on earth. The gothic cathedrals with their architecture soaring heavenward and our baroque churches in Upper Swabia are wonderful artistic expressions of this truth. It is not for nothing that people say that heaven is nearer in Upper Swabia!

Fortunately, a great deal has already been done to overcome the excessively sparse and modest celebration of the liturgy that we have all too often seen in the last few decades, where the Mass seemed to have no connection at all to human culture. It is one thing to get rid of false pomp, but to negate all culture is something completely different. We hear a lot today about the priest's *ars celebrandi,* the "art of celebrating." This is much more than simply an exhortation to observe the rubrics correctly; a dignified celebration and a liturgical culture should express the inner beauty of the eucharist. Ultimately, beauty is an attribute, an expression, and a reflection of God's own being, which is reflected in the beauty of the world and will one day transfigure the whole of reality. This is what the Bible means when it speaks of the glory of God (*kabôd, doxa*).

When God's beauty and glory are revealed in the celebration of the liturgy and bestow splendor on the Mass, a whole new world is disclosed to many people. A window is opened onto the other world of transcendence, giving a ray of hope in a world that many people experience as grey and leaden. Such a liturgy fascinates people, inviting them and attracting them. It kindles amazement, hope, and joy. As Saint Paul says in another context, outsiders who come to this worship will say: "God is really among you!" (I Cor 14:25).

– Conclusion –

Servant of Your Joy

Taken together, all these different aspects confirm my conviction that the priesthood is not obsolete. It will continue in the future to be a necessary service, one that heals the distress of humankind; and it is a worthwhile and beautiful ministry for the priest himself. Before the post-conciliar reform of the liturgy, we began the Mass each day with words from Psalm 42(43): *Et introibo ad altare Dei, ad Deum qui laetificat iuventutem meam,* "And I shall go in unto the altar of God, to the God who gives joy to my youth." These words remain true!

This brings us back at the end of this book to the theme of joy and to the task of being what Saint Paul calls a "servant of your joy." This is particularly important today: we must help as many people as possible to rediscover the true sources of joy, which means more than amusement or entertainment. These words are prompted by hostility to the body or to pleasure; I am not suggesting that we should do without all those harmless everyday pleasures that make life bearable and indeed worth living in human terms. Nothing is to be taken away, but something decisive is to be added. The Fourth Gospel speaks of the "perfecting" of our joy (John 15:11).

The everyday joys give us strength and a foretaste of true joy, since they whet our appetite for more—for a joy that is not ephemeral but remains. This is how Jesus argues in his conversation with the Samaritan woman at Jacob's well (John 4:13f.) and with the crowds who want to make him their king after the miraculous multiplication of the loaves (John 6:27, 35, 49-51, 54). I believe that this positive approach of Christian humanism remains the correct pastoral path today. We should not hunt out the weaknesses of human beings and attempt to make these the starting point of our pastoral work. It is better to begin with the great and beautiful things that already exist in life, and to use these to awaken the sense of delight in God.

Basically, the human person is born for joy. We all want to be happy. But where and how do we find happiness? Only God is great enough to fill to the full height and depth and the whole breadth of our heart. "God alone suffices," said Teresa of Avila. Augustine sums up the experience of his life in these words: "You have made us for your own self, and our heart is restless until it comes to rest in you" (*Confessions* I.I).

Augustine, with the whole philosophical and theological tradition, calls this "rest" *beatitudo*, which we usually translate as "bliss." This word however has primarily emotional overtones; it suggests a *feeling* of happiness, which, of course, exists—and which can certainly exist in the life of a priest. But reality usually pulls us pretty quickly back down to the ground; we cannot continue in such emotional states. *Beatitudo* belongs to the ultimate definition of what human existence is: we are created for the infinite happiness that we find only in God, when "we shall see him as he is" (I John 3:2). Augustine described this perfect joy as follows: "Then we shall rest and see—see and love—love and praise. That is what will be one day, in that end without end" (*City of God* 22.30).

We need not waste our energies on dreaming of this happiness, for it is not a matter of dreams. The Beatitudes of the Sermon on the Mount promise that we can find a joy that anticipates perfect happiness in situations that are very unpleasant in human terms (Matt 5:12; Luke 6:23). One who believes knows that he is already accepted definitively by the God in whose love his life is already perfectly safe. "Nothing can separate us from the love of God, which is in Christ Jesus our Lord" (Rom 8:39).

It would therefore be wrong to proclaim a message of woe and lamentation. It would be wrong to play funeral marches all the time. Ours is a message of the resurrection, of joy and of hope, and this means that we can look to the future with confidence—despite everything that weighs us down, and despite the occasional pessimistic prognosis that we hear.

With the Second Vatican Council, the church took the risk of setting out into a new period, and we are only at the beginning of this journey. No one can realistically expect *this* journey to be a pleasant little stroll. And naturally, the cross belongs to the ministry of the priest. Yet even now, his ministry is lit up by the transfiguring light of the resurrection. With the Easter message, he can bring orientation, light, consolation, trust, hope, and joy into the life of many people. He must bear witness that "The joy in the Lord is your strength" (Neh 8:10), and since this is so, the priest can be a "servant of your joy" (2 Cor 1:24) today—and in the future.

Index of Biblical Passages

Index of Names

187

Of Related Interest

CHRISTOPHER RUDDY

TESTED IN EVERY WAY

"Exemplary in its depth and bracing in its clarity."
—Kenneth L. Woodward,
Contributing Editor, *Newsweek*

In recent years, the Catholic priesthood in the United States has suffered numerous trials, from ever-diminishing numbers to the humiliations of the clerical sexual-abuse crisis. And, yet, by virtually every statistical measure, Catholic priests remain among the happiest of men. In *Tested in Every Way,* Christopher Ruddy examines this paradox, drawing on the insights of the "Priest in the Church" conference convened by the Catholic Common Ground Initiative. Ruddy moves beyond the cultural and theological impasses that paralyze the church and its mission to give us a vision of the priesthood that is both honest and hopeful.

0-8245-2427-6

crossroad

Of Related Interest

Joseph Cardinal Ratzinger (Pope Benedict XVI)

THE YES OF JESUS CHRIST

"Not 'eye for eye, tooth for tooth,' but the transformation of evil through the power of love. . . . Jesus bursts our No open by means of a stronger and greater Yes. In the cross of Christ and only there this saying opens up and becomes revelation. In fellowship with him, however, it becomes a possibility for our own life too." We are not allowed neutrality when faced with the question of God. We can only say Yes or No.

Secular thought has failed to answer the great questions of human existence. The "optimism" that lacks a Christian foundation ultimately cannot sustain genuine faith, hope, and love. In *The Yes of Jesus Christ,* Benedict XVI invites us to rediscover the Christian basis for hope. By exercising our spirituality through continual practice in Christian life, we hear again the distinctly Christian message that our ability to say Yes to ourselves and one another can only come from God's Yes in Christ.

Other Benedict XVI books available from Crossroad include *A New Song for the Lord: Faith in Christ and Liturgy Today.*

0-8245-2374-1

crossroad

Of Related Interest

WALTER CARDINAL KASPER

LEADERSHIP IN THE CHURCH

This book offers a timely and profound look at the enduring meaning of church office, and the guidance it is called to provide in light of a changed world and a challenging future. Topics addressed include: the universal vs. local church; the ministry of the bishop, priest and deacon; apostolic succession; and the practical application of canonical norms.

"One of the most important books in ecclesiology."
—*America Magazine*

0-8245-1977-9

At your bookstore or, to order directly from the publisher, please send check or money order (including $4.00 for the first book plus $1.00 for each additional book) to:

THE CROSSROAD PUBLISHING COMPANY
481 EIGHTH AVENUE, NEW YORK, NY 10001
1-800-707-0670 (toll free)

crossroad